The Obliga
Implementing the
SUNNAH
and Deeming Whoever
Rejects it of Disbelief

&

The Obligation of
Adhering to the Sunnah
and Being Wary of
INNOVATION

Shaykh 'Abdul 'Azīz bin 'Abdullāh
B I N B Ā Z
[1420AH] رَحِمَهُٱللَّه

© Maktabatulirshad Publications Ltd, USA

ISBN: 978-1-6420-4272-6

First Edition: Rabīʿ Awwal 1439 A.H. / December 2017 C.E.

Cover Design: Usul Designs

Translation by Mustapha Abdul Hakim Lameu Misrī

Revision & Editing by ʿAbdullāh Omrān

Typesetting & formatting by
Abū Sulaymān Muḥammad ʿAbdul-ʿAẓīm Ibn Joshua Baker

Printing: Ohio Printing

Subject: ʿAqīdah

Website: www.maktabatulirshad.com
E-mail: info@maktabatulirshad.com

مكتبة الإرشاد
Maktabatul-Irshad
PUBLICATIONS

Table of Contents

TRANSLITERATION TABLE

Consonants

ء	ʾ	د	d	ض	ḍ	ك	k
ب	b	ذ	dh	ط	ṭ	ل	l
ت	t	ر	r	ظ	ẓ	م	m
ث	th	ز	z	ع	ʿ	ن	n
ج	j	س	s	غ	gh	هـ	h
ح	ḥ	ش	sh	ف	f	و	w
خ	kh	ص	ṣ	ق	q	ي	y

Vowels

Short	َ	a	ِ	i	ُ	u
Long	ـَا	ā	ـِي	ī	ـُو	ū
Diphthongs	ـَو	aw	ـَي	ay		

ARABIC SYMBOLS & THEIR MEANINGS

حفظه الله	May Allāh preserve him
رَضِيَاللَّهُعَنْهُ	May Allāh be pleased with him (i.e., a male companion of the Prophet Muḥammad)
سُبْحَانَهُوَتَعَالَى	Glorified & Exalted is Allāh
عَزَّوَجَلَّ	(Allāh) the Mighty & Sublime
تَبَارَكَوَتَعَالَى	(Allāh) the Blessed & Exalted
جَلَّوَعَلَا	(Allāh) the Sublime & Exalted
عَلَيْهِالصَّلَاةُوَالسَّلَامُ	May Allāh send Blessings & Safety upon him (i.e., a Prophet or Messenger)

صَلَّى ٱللَّهُ عَلَيْهِ وَعَلَى آلِهِ وَسَلَّمَ

May Allāh send Blessings & Safety upon him and his family (i.e., Duʿā sent when mentioning the Prophet Muḥammad)

رَحِمَهُ ٱللَّهُ

May Allāh have mercy on him

رَضِىَ ٱللَّهُ عَنْهُمْ

May Allāh be pleased with them (i.e., Duʿā made for the Companions of the Prophet Muḥammad)

جَلَّ جَلَالُهُ

(Allāh) His Majesty is Exalted

رَضِىَ ٱللَّهُ عَنْهَا

May Allāh be pleased with her (i.e., a female companion of the Prophet Muḥammad)

THE OBLIGATION OF IMPLEMENTING THE SUNNAH AND DEEMING WHOEVER REJECTS IT OF DISBELIEF[1]

All praise belongs to Allāh and the final outcome and blesses end is for the pious. May Allāh raise the rank of His Servant and Messenger, our Prophet Muḥammad, who was sent as a mercy for all of mankind, jinn and all that exists. May Allāh raise the rank of his family, his companions who accurately and sincerely carried this religion with the best memorization of the meanings and words conveyed in the Book of Allāh and the Sunnah of the Prophet (ﷺ) as well as the following generations. May Allāh be pleased with them and make us from those who followed them exactly in faith.

As for what follows:

The scholars, in the past and present, agree upon the well-regarded principles pertaining to the

---

[1] It is published in the Magazine of Al-Buhūth Al-Islāmiyah, fifth edition, issued from Muḥarram to Jumāda ath-Thāniyah 1400 AH, it is published in little pamphlet from the General Presidency 1400 AH, the Saudi Arab Printing Company.

establishment of the Islāmic legislation and clarifying permissible and impermissible matters found in:

- ❖ the Book of Allāh which falsehood cannot approach it in front or behind.

- ❖ the Sunnah of the Prophet (ﷺ), who doesn't speak of (his own) desire, rather it is only a Revelation revealed to him.

- ❖ Then the consensus of the scholars of this Ummah.

However, there is disagreement among the scholars concerning other principles, the most significant of them is Qiyās[2]. The majority of scholars said it is an authoritative source as long as it includes all considered requirements. Evidence of these fundamentals are numerous; however, the prominent are the following three:

_____

[2] **TN:** deduction of Islāmic rulings by analogy.

The first fundamental is the Noble Book of Allāh. Our Lord's words (i.e., the Qurʾān) demonstrate the obligation of adhering to it, clinging to it, and not going beyond its set boundaries. Allāh (سُبْحَانَهُوَتَعَالَى) says,

﴿ ٱتَّبِعُواْ مَآ أُنزِلَ إِلَيْكُم مِّن رَّبِّكُمْ وَلَا تَتَّبِعُواْ مِن دُونِهِۦٓ أَوْلِيَآءَ قَلِيلًا مَّا تَذَكَّرُونَ ۝ ﴾

"Follow what has been sent down to you from your Lord (the Qurʾān and Prophet Muḥammad's Sunnah), and follow not any Awliyā (protectors and helpers who order you to associate partners in worship with Allāh), besides Him (Allāh). Little do you remember!" [*Sūrah al-ʿArāf* 7:3]

Allāh also says,

﴿ وَهَٰذَا كِتَٰبٌ أَنزَلْنَٰهُ مُبَارَكٌ فَٱتَّبِعُوهُ وَٱتَّقُواْ لَعَلَّكُمْ تُرْحَمُونَ ۝ ﴾

"And this is a blessed Book (the Qurʾān) which We have sent down, so follow it and

fear Allāh (i.e., do not disobey His Orders), that you may receive mercy (i.e., be saved from the torment of Hell)." [*Sūrah al-'An'ām* 6:155]

and Allāh (سُبْحَانَهُ وَتَعَالَى) says,

$$﴿ قَدْ جَآءَكُم مِّنَ ٱللَّهِ نُورٌ وَكِتَـٰبٌ مُّبِينٌ ۞ يَهْدِى بِهِ ٱللَّهُ مَنِ ٱتَّبَعَ رِضْوَٰنَهُۥ سُبُلَ ٱلسَّلَـٰمِ وَيُخْرِجُهُم مِّنَ ٱلظُّلُمَـٰتِ إِلَى ٱلنُّورِ بِإِذْنِهِۦ وَيَهْدِيهِمْ إِلَىٰ صِرَٰطٍ مُّسْتَقِيمٍ ۞ ﴾$$

"Indeed, there has come to you from Allāh a light (Prophet Muḥammad (صَلَّى ٱللَّهُ عَلَيْهِ وَسَلَّمَ)) and a plain book (this Qur'ān). Wherewith Allāh guides all those who seek His Good Pleasure to ways of peace, and He brings them out of darkness by His Will to light and guides them to the Straight Way (Islāmic Monotheism)." [*Sūrah al-Mā'idah* 5:15-16]

and Allāh (سُبْحَانَهُ وَتَعَالَى) says,

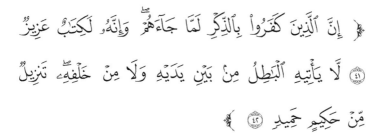

"Verily, those who disbelieved in the Reminder (i.e., the Qurʾān) when it came to them (shall receive the punishment). And verily, it is an honorable well-fortified respected Book (because it is Allāh's Speech, and He has protected it from corruption). Falsehood cannot come to it from before it or behind it: (it is) sent down by the All-Wise, Worthy of all praise (Allāh عَزَّوَجَلَّ)." [*Sūrah Fussilāt* 41:41-42]

and Allāh (عَزَّوَجَلَّ) says,

﴿ وَأُوحِيَ إِلَيَّ هَٰذَا ٱلْقُرْءَانُ لِأُنذِرَكُم بِهِۦ وَمَنۢ بَلَغَ ﴾

"This Qurʾān has been revealed to me that I may therewith warn you and whomsoever it may reach." [*Sūrah al-ʾAnʿām* 6:19]

and Allāh (سُبْحَانَهُوَتَعَالَى) says,

﴿ هَٰذَا بَلَٰغٌ لِّلنَّاسِ وَلِيُنذَرُوا۟ بِهِۦ ﴾

"This (Qur'ān) is a Message for mankind (and a clear proof against them), in order that they may be warned thereby." [*Sūrah Ibrāhīm* 14:52]

There are many verses in this respect.

There are authentic aḥādīth from the Messenger of Allāh (صَلَّىٰاللَّهُعَلَيْهِوَسَلَّمَ) which order sticking and adhering to the Qur'ān. These aḥādīth demonstrate that whoever sticks to the Qur'ān will be guided, and whoever abandons it will be led astray. An example of that is what the Prophet (صَلَّىٰاللَّهُعَلَيْهِوَسَلَّمَ) said in his farewell pilgrimage speech,

إِنِّي تَارِكٌ فِيكُمْ مَا لَنْ تُضِلُّوا إِنِ اعْتَصَمْتُمْ بِهِ كِتَابُ اللهِ

"Indeed, I have left among you, that which if you keep steadfast upon it, you shall not be led astray, the Book of Allāh." related by Muslim in Saḥīḥ.

It related by Muslim also on the authority of Zayd ibn Arqam (رَضِيَاللَّهُعَنْهُ), the Prophet (صَلَّىٰاللَّهُعَلَيْهِوَسَلَّمَ) said,

تَارِكٌ فِيكُمْ ثَقَلَيْنِ أَوَّلُهُمَا كِتَابُ اللَّهِ فِيهِ الْهُدَى وَالنُّورُ فَخُذُوا بِكِتَابِ اللَّهِ وَاسْتَمْسِكُوا بِهِ فَحَثَّ عَلَى كِتَابِ اللَّهِ وَرَغَّبَ فِيهِ ثُمَّ قَالَ " وَأَهْلُ بَيْتِي أُذَكِّرُكُمُ اللَّهَ فِي أَهْلِ بَيْتِي أُذَكِّرُكُمُ اللَّهَ فِي أَهْلِ بَيْتِي أُذَكِّرُكُمُ اللَّهَ فِي أَهْلِ بَيْتِي

"I will leave two most valuable things, first of all, is the Book of Allāh, in which there are right guidance and light, so stick to the Book of Allāh and adhere to it. He exhorted us to hold fast to the Book of Allāh and then said: The second are the members of my family I remind you of (your duties) to the members of my family."

In another narration, he said, concerning the Qurʾān,

هُوَ حَبْلُ اللهِ مَنْ تَمَسَّكَ بِهِ كَانَ عَلَى الْـهُدَى وَ تَرَكَهُ كَانَ عَلَى الضَّلَالِ

"It is the Rope of Allāh whoever holds fast to it will be upon guidance, and whoever abandons it will be upon misguidance."

In this respect, there are numerous ahādīth.

In addition, there is the consensus of the people of knowledge and faith from the Companions and who follow them along with the Sunnah of the Messenger of Allāh (ﷺ) which indicates the obligation of sticking to the Book Allāh, ruling according to it, and settling disputes based upon it. All of this evidence is sufficient instead of not going in more details.

The second fundamental of the three fundamentals agreed upon is the authentic ahādīth of the Messenger of Allāh (ﷺ), and the companions and the people of knowledge and faith who follow them, all of them believe in this great fundamental and consider it as evidence, and teach it the Ummah.

So, they compiled many books and clarified this in the books of Usul Fiqh and Muṣṭalaḥ, upon which there is much evidence. The Noble Qur'ān urges the Muslims in the Prophet's lifetime and the coming generations to follow and comply with it. Because he was sent to all of mankind and Jinn, and they should follow and obey him until the Day of Judgment. The Messenger of Allāh (ﷺ) is the one who explained and clarified in his sayings, deeds, and declarations what is summed up in the Book of Allāh. The Sunnah of the Prophet (ﷺ) explains in detail the Rakaʿāt of the prayers, how to pray, and what is obligatory in it. Without the Sunnah the Muslims wouldn't know the details of fasting, Zakat, Hajj, Jihād, enjoining the good and forbidding the evil, rulings of transactions and forbidden things, and punishments and limits set by Allāh.

The ayahs which refer to this matter are mentioned in ʾĀli ʿImrān,

$$﴿ وَأَطِيعُوا۟ ٱللَّهَ وَٱلرَّسُولَ لَعَلَّكُمْ تُرْحَمُونَ ۝ ﴾$$

"And obey Allāh and the Messenger (Muḥammad (ﷺ)) that you may obtain mercy." [Sūrah ʾĀli ʿImrān 3:132]

and in Surah An-Nisāʾ,

$$﴿ يَٰٓأَيُّهَا ٱلَّذِينَ ءَامَنُوٓا۟ أَطِيعُوا۟ ٱللَّهَ وَأَطِيعُوا۟ ٱلرَّسُولَ وَأُو۟لِى$$

$$ٱلْأَمْرِ مِنكُمْ فَإِن تَنَٰزَعْتُمْ فِى شَىْءٍ فَرُدُّوهُ إِلَى ٱللَّهِ وَٱلرَّسُولِ إِن$$

كُنتُمْ تُؤْمِنُونَ بِٱللَّهِ وَٱلْيَوْمِ ٱلْأَخِرِ ذَٰلِكَ خَيْرٌ وَأَحْسَنُ
تَأْوِيلًا ۞

"O you who believe! Obey Allāh and obey the Messenger (Muḥammad (ﷺ)), and those of you (Muslims) who are in authority. And if you differ in anything amongst yourselves, refer it to Allāh and His Messenger ((ﷺ)) if you believe in Allāh and in the Last Day. That is better and more suitable for final determination." [*Sūrah an-Nisā'* 4:59]

Allāh (سُبْحَانَهُوَتَعَالَى) also says in Sūrah An-Nisā',

﴿ مَّن يُطِعِ ٱلرَّسُولَ فَقَدْ أَطَاعَ ٱللَّهَ وَمَن تَوَلَّىٰ فَمَآ
أَرْسَلْنَٰكَ عَلَيْهِمْ حَفِيظًا ۞ ﴾

"He who obeys the Messenger (Muḥammad (ﷺ)), has indeed obeyed Allāh, but he who turns away, then we have not sent you (O

Muḥammad (ﷺ)) as a watcher over them." [*Sūrah an-Nisāʾ* 4:80]

How is possible to obey him (ﷺ), refer disputes amongst the people to the Book of Allāh and the Sunnah of His Messenger (ﷺ) if the Sunnah is not used as a pretext or all of it is not preserved. So, based upon that (statement) Allāh guided the people to something which doesn't exist, and this is a fallacy, among the greatest forms of disbelief and mistrust in Allāh., Allāh (ﷻ) says,

$$ وَأَنزَلْنَآ إِلَيْكَ ٱلذِّكْرَ لِتُبَيِّنَ لِلنَّاسِ مَا نُزِّلَ إِلَيْهِمْ وَلَعَلَّهُمْ يَتَفَكَّرُونَ ﴿٤٤﴾ $$

"And We have also sent down to you (O Muḥammad (ﷺ)) the Dhikr [reminder and the advice (i.e., the Qurʾān)], that you may explain clearly to men what is sent down to them, and that they may give thought." [*Sūrah an-Nahl* 16:44]

and Allāh (ﷻ) says,

﴿ وَمَآ أَنزَلْنَا عَلَيْكَ ٱلْكِتَٰبَ إِلَّا لِتُبَيِّنَ لَهُمُ ٱلَّذِى ٱخْتَلَفُوا۟ فِيهِ وَهُدًى وَرَحْمَةً لِّقَوْمٍ يُؤْمِنُونَ ۝ ﴾

"And We have not sent down the Book (the Qur'ān) to you (O Muḥammad (ﷺ)), except that you may explain clearly to them those things in which they differ, and (as) a guidance and a mercy for a folk who believe."
[*Sūrah an-Nahl* 16:64]

So, how would Allāh entrust His Messenger (ﷺ) to explain what has been revealed to them (i.e., Qur'ān) and his Sunnah doesn't exist or has no basis! An example of that is mentioned in Sūrah An-Nūr:

﴿ قُلْ أَطِيعُوا۟ ٱللَّهَ وَأَطِيعُوا۟ ٱلرَّسُولَ فَإِن تَوَلَّوْا۟ فَإِنَّمَا عَلَيْهِ مَا حُمِّلَ وَعَلَيْكُم مَّا حُمِّلْتُمْ وَإِن تُطِيعُوهُ تَهْتَدُوا۟ وَمَا عَلَى ٱلرَّسُولِ إِلَّا ٱلْبَلَٰغُ ٱلْمُبِينُ ۝ ﴾

"Say: "Obey Allāh and obey the Messenger ((ﷺ)), but if you turn away, he (Messenger Muḥammad (ﷺ)) is only responsible for the duty placed on him (i.e., to convey Allāh's Message) and you for that placed on you. If you obey him, you shall be on the right guidance. The Messenger's duty is only to convey (the message) in a clear way (i.e., to preach in a plain way)." [*Sūrah an-Nūr* 24:54]

and Allāh (سُبْحَانَهُوَتَعَالَ) says in the same Sūrah,

﴿ وَأَقِيمُواْ ٱلصَّلَوٰةَ وَءَاتُواْ ٱلزَّكَوٰةَ وَأَطِيعُواْ ٱلرَّسُولَ لَعَلَّكُمْ تُرْحَمُونَ ٥٦ ﴾

"And perform As-Ṣalāh (Iqamat-as-Ṣalāh), and give Zakat and obey the Messenger (Muḥammad (ﷺ)) that you may receive mercy (from Allāh)." [*Sūrah an-Nūr* 24:56]

Allāh (عَزَّوَجَلَّ) also says in Sūrah Al-'Arāf,

﴿ قُل يَـٰٓأَيُّهَا ٱلنَّاسُ إِنِّي رَسُولُ ٱللَّهِ إِلَيۡكُمۡ جَمِيعًا

ٱلَّذِى لَهُۥ مُلۡكُ ٱلسَّمَـٰوَٰتِ وَٱلۡأَرۡضِ لَآ إِلَـٰهَ إِلَّا هُوَ

يُحۡىِۦ وَيُمِيتُ فَـَٔامِنُواْ بِٱللَّهِ وَرَسُولِهِ ٱلنَّبِيِّ ٱلۡأُمِّيِّ ٱلَّذِى

يُؤۡمِنُ بِٱللَّهِ وَكَلِمَـٰتِهِۦ وَٱتَّبِعُوهُ لَعَلَّكُمۡ

تَهۡتَدُونَ ۝ (١٥٨) ﴾

"Say: (O Muḥammad (ﷺ)): "O
mankind! Verily, I am sent to you all as the
Messenger of Allāh – to Whom belongs the
dominion of the heavens and the earth. La
ilaha illa Huwa (none has the right to be
worshipped but He). It is He Who gives life
and causes death. So, believe in Allāh and His
Messenger (Muḥammad (ﷺ)), the
Prophet who can neither read nor write (i.e.
Muḥammad (ﷺ)), who believes in
Allāh and His Words [(this Qurʾān), the
Taurat (Torah) and the Injeel (Gospel) and
also Allāh's Word: "Be!"- and he was, i.e. 'Isa
(Jesus) son of Maryam (Mary), عَلَيۡهِمَاٱلسَّلَامُ], and

follow him so that you may be guided." [*Sūrah al-ʿArāf* 7:158]

These Ayāt indicate clearly that guidance and mercy lie in adhering to the Prophet (ﷺ). How is this possible without implementation of his Sunnah, or saying it is unauthentic or unreliable?

Allāh (سُبْحَانَهُۥوَتَعَالَىٰ) says in Sūrah An-Nūr,

﴿ فَلْيَحْذَرِ ٱلَّذِينَ يُخَالِفُونَ عَنْ أَمْرِهِۦٓ أَن تُصِيبَهُمْ فِتْنَةٌ أَوْ يُصِيبَهُمْ عَذَابٌ أَلِيمٌ ٦٣ ﴾

"And let those who oppose the Messenger's (Muḥammad (ﷺ)) commandment (i.e., his Sunnah – legal ways, orders, acts of worship, statements) (among the sects) beware, let some Fitnah (disbelief, trials, afflictions, earthquakes, killing, overpowered by a tyrant) should befall them or a painful torment be inflicted on them." [*Sūrah an-Nūr* 24:63]

and Allāh says in Sūrah Al-Hashr,

﴿ وَمَا ءَاتَىٰكُمُ ٱلرَّسُولُ فَخُذُوهُ وَمَا نَهَىٰكُمْ عَنْهُ
فَٱنتَهُوٓا۟ ﴾

"And whatsoever the Messenger (Muḥammad (ﷺ)) gives you, take it; and whatsoever he forbids you, abstain (from it)." [*Sūrah al-Hashr* 59:7]

In this regard, many verses indicate the obligation of obeying the Prophet and adhering to his Sunnah. Also, previous evidence indicated the obligation of adhering to the Book of Allāh, sticking to it, and complying with his orders and abstaining from its prohibitions. These are two relevant fundamentals in which whoever denies one of them denies the other. This is considered an act of disbelief and misguidance which takes one outside the fold of Islām as agreed by all the scholars.

The aḥādīth of the Prophet (ﷺ) indicated the obligation of obeying the Messenger of Allāh (ﷺ), following his Sunnah and refraining from disobeying him. All of this is relative to the people of his era as well as those to come. It is related by Al-Bukhārī, and Muslim on the authority of Abū Hurayrah (رَضِيَٱللَّهُعَنْهُ) the Prophet (صَلَّىٱللَّهُعَلَيْهِوَسَلَّمَ) said,

مَنْ أَطَاعَنِي فَقَدْ أَطَاعَ اللَّهَ، وَمَنْ عَصَانِي فَقَدْ عَصَى اللَّهَ

"whosoever obeys me, obeys Allāh; and he who disobeys me disobeys Allāh."

It is related by Al-Bukhārī on the authority of Abū Hurayrah (رَضِيَٱللَّهُعَنْهُ) also that the Prophet (صَلَّىٱللَّهُعَلَيْهِوَسَلَّمَ) said,

كُلُّ أُمَّتِي يَدْخُلُونَ الْجَنَّةَ، إِلاَّ مَنْ أَبَى ". قَالُوا يَا رَسُولَ اللهِ وَمَنْ يَأْبَى قَالَ " مَنْ أَطَاعَنِي دَخَلَ الْجَنَّةَ، وَمَنْ عَصَانِي فَقَدْ أَبَى

"Every one of my Ummah will enter Jannah except those who refuse." He was asked: "who will refuse?" He (صَلَّىٱللَّهُعَلَيْهِوَسَلَّمَ) said: "Whoever obeys me, shall enter Jannah, and whosoever disobeys me, refuses to (enter Jannah)."

It is also related by 'Aḥmad, Abū Dawud and Al-Hakim on the authority of Al-Miqdām Ibn Maʿdī Karib that the Messenger of Allāh (صَلَّىٱللَّهُعَلَيْهِوَسَلَّمَ) said,

أَلاَ إِنِّي أُوتِيتُ الْكِتَابَ وَمِثْلَهُ مَعَهُ أَلاَ يُوشِكُ رَجُلٌ شَبْعَانُ عَلَى أَرِيكَتِهِ يَقُولُ عَلَيْكُمْ بِهَذَا الْقُرْآنِ فَمَا وَجَدْتُمْ فِيهِ مِنْ حَلاَلٍ فَأَحِلُّوهُ وَمَا وَجَدْتُمْ فِيهِ مِنْ حَرَامٍ فَحَرِّمُوهُ

"Beware! I have been given the Qur'ān and something like it, yet the time is coming when a man replete on his couch will say: keep to the Qur'ān; what you find in it to be permissible treat as permissible, and what you find in it to be prohibited treat as prohibited."

Related by Abū Dawud and Ibn Majah with an authentic chain of narration on the authority of Abū Rafi' that the Prophet (ﷺ) said,

لاَ أُلْفِيَنَّ أَحَدَكُمْ مُتَّكِئًا عَلَى أَرِيكَتِهِ يَأْتِيهِ الأَمْرُ مِنْ أَمْرِي مِمَّا أَمَرْتُ بِهِ أَوْ نَهَيْتُ عَنْهُ فَيَقُولُ لاَ نَدْرِي مَا وَجَدْنَا فِي كِتَابِ اللَّهِ اتَّبَعْنَاهُ

"Let me not find one of you reclining on his couch when he hears something regarding my

Sunnah which I have commanded or forbidden saying: I have no knowledge of that. What we found in Allāh's Book we have followed."

On the authority of Al-Hassan Ibn Jabir,

يُوشِكُ الرَّجُلُ مُتَّكِئًا عَلَى أَرِيكَتِهِ يُحَدَّثُ بِحَدِيثٍ مِنْ حَدِيثِي فَيَقُولُ بَيْنَنَا وَبَيْنَكُمْ كِتَابُ اللهِ عَزَّ وَجَلَّ فَمَا وَجَدْنَا فِيهِ مِنْ حَلَالٍ اسْتَحْلَلْنَاهُ وَمَا وَجَدْنَا فِيهِ مِنْ حَرَامٍ حَرَّمْنَاهُ . أَلاَ وَإِنَّ مَا حَرَّمَ رَسُولُ اللهِ ـ صلى الله عليه وسلم ـ مِثْلُ مَا حَرَّمَ اللَّهُ

I heard Al-Miqdām Ibn Maʿdī Karib (رَضِيَٱللَّهُعَنْهُ) saying: The Messenger of Allāh (صَلَّىٱللَّهُعَلَيْهِوَسَلَّمَ) has forbidden some things on the Day of Khaybar then he (صَلَّىٱللَّهُعَلَيْهِوَسَلَّمَ) said: "soon there will come a time that one accuses me of lying whereas he was reclining on his couch telling about my Sunnah, saying the Book of Allāh is between us. Whatever it states is permissible, we will take as permissible, and whatever it states is forbidden, we will take as forbidden. verily, whatever the Messenger of Allāh (سُبْحَانَهُوَتَعَالَى) has forbidden is like that which

Allāh (سُبْحَانَهُوَتَعَالَى) has forbidden." related by Al-Hakim, At-Tirmidhi and Ibn Majah with an authentic chain of narration.

The ahādīth of the Messenger of Allāh (صَلَّىَاللَّهُعَلَيْهِوَسَلَّمَ) has reached the level being reported from a number of Companions that He (صَلَّىَاللَّهُعَلَيْهِوَسَلَّمَ) would advise his companions in sermons that those who are present should convey to those who are absent saying,

رُبَّ مُبَلِّغٍ يُبَلِّغُهُ أَوْعَى لَهُ مِنْ سَامِعٍ

"For perhaps the one to whom it is conveyed to will understand it better than the one who (first) hears it."

Also, it is related by Al-Bukhārī and Muslim that when the Prophet (صَلَّىَاللَّهُعَلَيْهِوَسَلَّمَ) delivered a speech in farewell Hajj on the Day of Arafah and on the Day of Sacrifice, he (صَلَّىَاللَّهُعَلَيْهِوَسَلَّمَ) said,

فَلْيُبَلِّغْ الشَّاهِدُ الْغَائِبَ، فَرُبَّ مَنْ يُبَلِّغُهُ أَوْعَى لَهُ مِمَّنْ سَمِعَهُ

"Let those who are present convey to those who are absent. For perhaps the one to whom

it is conveyed to will understand it better than the one who (first) hears it."

If his Sunnah is not a plea against who heard it and whom it was conveyed to, if it didn't remain until the Day of Judgment, and he (صَلَّى ٱللَّهُ عَلَيْهِ وَسَلَّمَ) didn't order it to be conveyed then it can be deducted from that the Sunnah is an established Hujjah upon those who heard it from the mouth of him (صَلَّى ٱللَّهُ عَلَيْهِ وَسَلَّمَ) as well as those whom it was transmitted to with an authentic chain of narrators.

The companions of the Messenger of Allāh (صَلَّى ٱللَّهُ عَلَيْهِ وَسَلَّمَ) has memorized his oral and verbal Sunnah, and conveyed to the Tābi'īn who conveyed to the following generations; the trusted scholars transmitted the Sunnah over generations, compiled books of the Sunnah, distinguished the authentic from the unauthentic. They set rules and laws to clarify the Sunnah. The scholars have circulated and preserved the Sunnah books including two most authentic books (Bukhārī and Muslim). Allāh (سُبْحَانَهُ وَتَعَالَى) preserved his Noble Book and guarded it against those who belie or make distortions as indicated by Allāh (سُبْحَانَهُ وَتَعَالَى),

"Verily, We, it is We Who have sent down the Dhikr (i.e., the Qur'ān) and surely, We will guard it (against corruption)." [*Sūrah al-Hijr* 15:9]

There is no doubt that the Sunnah of the Messenger of Allāh (ﷺ) is revelation sent down. So, Allāh (عَزَّوَجَلَّ) preserved it just like He preserved His book. Allāh (سُبْحَانَهُوَتَعَالَى) dedicated critical scholars who would keep the Sunnah from being distorted and misinterpreted by the ignorant. Those scholars guarded it against corruption made by the ignorant and liars because Allāh (سُبْحَانَهُوَتَعَالَى) considered it, the Sunnah, an explanation of His Noble Book. The Sunnah is a clarification for the Qur'ān's summarized rulings, other rulings in the Sunnah which is not found in the Noble Qur'ān, detail rulings as it relates to breastfeeding, some rulings concerning inheritance, prohibition of combining the woman and her maternal and paternal aunt in marriage, and many other rulings stated in the Sunnah but not mentioned in the Noble Qurʾān.

Regarding what is mentioned by the companions, their followers and the following scholars about dignifying the Sunnah and the obligation of adherence to it. It is related in the two most authentic books (Bukhārī and Muslim) on the authority of Abū Hurayrah (رَضِوَٱللَّهُعَنْهُ),

"When the Messenger of Allāh (صَلَّىٱللَّهُعَلَيْهِوَسَلَّمَ) was dead, and the Arabs turned back from Islām, Abū Bakr As-Siddiq (رَضِوَٱللَّهُعَنْهُ) said: "I will fight who make a difference between the ruling of Ṣalāh and Zakat," ʿUmar (رَضِوَٱللَّهُعَنْهُ) replied: "how can you fight them, whereas the Prophet (صَلَّىٱللَّهُعَلَيْهِوَسَلَّمَ) said: "I have been commanded to fight against the people so long as they do not declare that there is none has the right to be worshipped but Allāh, and whoever declared this his property and life will be protected on my behalf except for the right affairs?" by Allāh, if they withhold from me a young goat that they used to give to the Messenger of Allāh (سُبْحَانَهُوَتَعَالَى), I will fight them for withholding it. ʿUmar (رَضِوَٱللَّهُعَنْهُ) said:

"By Allāh, as soon as I realized that Allāh had expanded the chest of Abū Bakr to fight them, I knew that it was the truth."

The companions (رَضِيَاللهُعَنْهُمْ) has fought against those who turned their backs on Islām and fought against those who insisted upon that. This story proves the obligation of the Sunnah and attaching significant importance to it. Furthermore, when the grandmother came to As-Siddiq (رَضِيَاللهُعَنْهُ) asking about her inheritance, he replied: "nothing is found in the Book of Allāh regarding your inheritance, and I do not know if the Messenger of Allāh (صَلَّىاللهُعَلَيْهِوَسَلَّمَ) gave any ruling in this respect, but I will ask about that." Then he asked the companions (رَضِيَاللهُعَنْهُمْ); some said that the Prophet (صَلَّىاللهُعَلَيْهِوَسَلَّمَ) had given the grandmother a sixth (of the inheritance). So, Abū Bakr Siddiq gave a ruling giving her that portion. Moreover, 'Umar (رَضِيَاللهُعَنْهُ) has ordered the rulers to decide judicially between the people using the Book of Allāh, if not a ruling was not found in there then look in the Sunnah of the Messenger of Allāh (صَلَّىاللهُعَلَيْهِوَسَلَّمَ). Also, when the case of stillbirth was presented in 'Umar's time, in which her baby was stillborn because being attacked by someone. ʿUmar asked the companions about this; so Muḥammad ibn Maslammah and Al-Mughīrah Ibn Shuʿbah (رَضِيَٱللَّهُعَنْهُمَا) said that the Prophet (صَلَّىٱللَّهُعَلَيْهِوَسَلَّمَ) gave a ruling to give a male or female slave, so ʿUmar (رَضِيَٱللَّهُعَنْهُ) made the same ruling.

When the case of observing the prescribed retreat of the waiting period after husband's death was presented at the time of ʿUthmān (رَضِيَٱللَّهُعَنْهُ), he was told by Furaiya Bint Malik ibn Sinan, the sister of Abū Said (رَضِيَٱللَّهُعَنْهُمَا) that the Prophet (صَلَّىٱللَّهُعَلَيْهِوَسَلَّمَ) ordered her after her husband's death to stay in his house till the waiting period is over, then he (رَضِيَٱللَّهُعَنْهُ) made the same ruling. Also, he gave the ruling according to the Sunnah regarding e carrying out punishment against the drunken. Also, when ʿAli (رَضِيَٱللَّهُعَنْهُ) heard that ʿUthmān (رَضِيَٱللَّهُعَنْهُ) forbade Hajj-at-Tamattu', ʿAli (رَضِيَٱللَّهُعَنْهُ) has pronounced Talbiyah of Hajj and Umrah together and said: "I cannot leave the Sunnah of the Messenger of Allāh aside for the sake of anyone."

When some people mentioned the opinion of Abū Bakr and ʿUmar (رَضِيَٱللَّهُعَنْهُمَا) regarding performing Hajj alone as an evidence before Ibn ʿAbbās (رَضِيَاللهُعَنْهُمَا), he said: "Soon stones will fall from the sky upon you (as a punishment), I said: The Messenger of Allāh (صَلَّىاللهُعَلَيْهِوَسَلَّم) said, but you said: Abū Bakr and ʿUmar said (opposing the saying of the Prophet).

So, when the Sunnah is opposed for the sake of Abū Bakr's and ʿUmar's opinions, one would be punished, what about those who opposed the Sunnah of the Prophet (صَلَّىاللهُعَلَيْهِوَسَلَّم) for the sake of lesser than them, or according to his own opinion!

When someone argued with ʿAbdullāh Ibn ʿUmar in doing the Sunnah of the Prophet (mentioning an opinion of ʿUmar), he said, "Are we order to follow ʿUmar or the Sunnah of the Prophet (صَلَّىاللهُعَلَيْهِوَسَلَّم)?"

When a man said to ʿImrān Ibn Hussain (رَضِيَاللهُعَنْهُمَا): "tell us about the verses from the Book of Allāh, while he is telling us about aḥādith of the Prophet" he (ʿImrān) became angry and said: "Sunnah is the Explanation of the Book of Allāh, without the Sunnah, no one will know that Dhuhr is a four-Rakaʿāt prayers, and Maghrib is three Rakaʿāt prayers, and Fajr is two Rakaʿāt prayers, no one will know about the rulings of Zakat, all these detailed rulings are mentioned in the Sunnah."

There are many sayings of the companions that attached significant importance to the Sunnah, the obligation of implementing it and warning against opposing it. When ʿAbdullāh Ibn ʿUmar mentioned a hadith:

لاَ تَمْنَعُوا إِمَاءَ اللَّهِ مَسَاجِدَ اللَّهِ

"Do not prevent the maid-servants of Allāh from going to the Masjid."

One of his sons said:

"By Allāh! we will prevent them" ʿAbdullāh became angry with him and severely insulted him, and said: "I said that the Messenger of Allāh (صَلَّى اللَّهُ عَلَيْهِ وَسَلَّمَ) said and you said: we will prevent them."

When ʿAbdullāh Ibn Al-Mughaffal Al-Muzanni (رَضِيَ اللَّهُ عَنْهُ), one of the Prophet's companions, saw one of his relatives throwing pebbles, he said: "the Messenger of Allāh (صَلَّى اللَّهُ عَلَيْهِ وَسَلَّمَ) prohibited throwing pebbles saying:

إِنَّهُ لاَ يَصِيدُ صَيْدًا وَلاَ يَنْكَأُ عَدُوًّا وَإِنَّمَا يَفْقَأُ الْعَيْنَ وَيَكْسِرُ
السِّنَّ

"prey is not caught by such means, neither is an enemy injured, but it may break a tooth, or gouge out someone's eye."

Then he saw him again throwing pebbles; he said:

"by Allāh, I will never speak to you again, though I told you that the Prophet (ﷺ) forbade throwing pebbles, you did it again."

Al-Bayhaqī related that Ayūb As-Sakhtiyānī, the great Tābī', said:

"If you tell someone about the Sunnah, and he says: do not tell us about the Sunnah, tell us about the Qurʾān. Then know that he is misguided."

Al-Awzaʾi (رَحِمَهُ اللّٰهُ) said:

"The Sunnah is a judge for the Book of Allāh. It specifies what is generalized in the Qurʾān or cites rulings not mentioned in the Book of Allāh just as Allāh (سُبْحَانَهُوَتَعَالَى) says,

﴿ وَأَنزَلْنَآ إِلَيْكَ ٱلذِّكْرَ لِتُبَيِّنَ لِلنَّاسِ مَا نُزِّلَ إِلَيْهِمْ وَلَعَلَّهُمْ يَتَفَكَّرُونَ ۝ ﴾

"And We have also sent down to you (O Muḥammad (صَلَّىٱللَّهُعَلَيْهِوَسَلَّمَ)) the Dhikr [reminder and the advice (i.e., the Qurʾān)], that you may explain clearly to men what is sent down to them, and that they may give thought." [*Sūrah an-Nahl* 16:44]

And the Messenger of Allāh (صَلَّىٱللَّهُعَلَيْهِوَسَلَّمَ) said,

أَلاَ إِنِّي أُوتِيتُ الْكِتَابَ وَمِثْلَهُ مَعَهُ

"I have been given the Book of Allāh and what is similar to it (the Sunnah)."

Al-Bayhaqī related on the authority of ʿĀmir Ash-Shābi (رَحِمَهُٱللَّهُ) who told some people,

"You went astray when you abandoned ahādīth." meaning the authentic Sunnah.

Al-Bayhaqī related on the authority of Al-Awza'i (رَحِمَهُٱللَّهُ) that he said to some of his students:

"When a hadith of the Messenger of Allāh (صَلَّىٱللَّهُعَلَيْهِوَسَلَّمَ) is conveyed to be wary not to say, 'someone else said' for indeed the Messenger of Allāh (صَلَّىٱللَّهُعَلَيْهِوَسَلَّمَ) conveyer sent by Allāh (سُبْحَانَهُوَتَعَالَ)."

Al-Bayhaqī related on the authority of great Imām, Sufyan Ibn Saʿīd Ath-Thawri (رَحِمَهُٱللَّهُ) who said,

"knowledge is based wholly upon ahādīth."

And Malik (رَحِمَهُٱللَّهُ) said,

"Everyone's statement can be argued against and refuted against except the person of this grave." He was pointing to the grave of the Messenger of Allāh (صَلَّىٱللَّهُعَلَيْهِوَسَلَّمَ).

Abū Hanīfah (رَحِمَهُٱللَّهُ) said,

"When the Ḥadīth reported by the Messenger of Allāh (صَلَّىٱللَّهُعَلَيْهِوَسَلَّمَ) is mentioned we should accept it."

Ash-Shāfiʿī (رَحِمَهُٱللَّه) said,

"If I narrated an authentic Ḥadīth of the Messenger of Allāh (صَلَّىٱللَّهُعَلَيْهِوَسَلَّمَ) and I don't follow it, know for sure that I have gone mad."

He (رَحِمَهُٱللَّه) also said,

"If I say a statement and there is a Ḥadīth that opposes it then throw my statement against the wall."

Imam ʾAḥmad ibn Hanbal (رَحِمَهُٱللَّه) said to some of his students,

"Do not imitate me, nor Mālik, nor Ash-Shāfiʿī, rather take from where have taken from (the Sunnah)."

He (رَحِمَهُٱللَّه) also said:

"How strange is that people know the chain of narration and its authenticity, but then follow Sufyān's opinion."

Allāh (سُبْحَانَهُوَتَعَالَى) says,

﴿ فَلْيَحْذَرِ ٱلَّذِينَ يُخَالِفُونَ عَنْ أَمْرِهِۦٓ أَن تُصِيبَهُمْ
فِتْنَةٌ أَوْ يُصِيبَهُمْ عَذَابٌ أَلِيمٌ ٦٣ ﴾

"And let those who oppose the Messenger's (Muḥammad (ﷺ)) commandment (i.e., his Sunnah – legal ways, orders, acts of worship, statements) (among the sects) beware, lest some Fitnah (disbelief, trials, afflictions, earthquakes, killing, overpowered by a tyrant) should befall them or a painful torment be inflicted on them." [*Sūrah an-Nūr* 24:63]

Then he (رَحِمَهُ ٱللَّهُ) said,

"do you know the meaning of Fitnah? Fitnah means Shirk. Thus he may be led astray if he opposed the sayings of Messenger of Allāh (صَلَّى ٱللَّهُ عَلَيْهِ وَسَلَّمَ)."

It is related by Al-Bayhaqī on the authority of Mujahid ibn Jābir, the Tābī', who commented on Allāh's (سُبْحَانَهُ وَتَعَالَىٰ) statement,

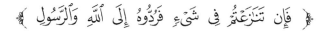

"And if you differ in anything amongst yourselves, refer it to Allāh and His Messenger ((ﷺ))." [*Sūrah an-Nisā'* 4:59]

He said,

"Referring it to Allāh means referring to His Book, and referring to the Messenger of Allāh means referring to the Sunnah."

Also, it is related by Al-Bayhaqī on the authority of Az-Zuhrī (رَحِمَهُٱللَّه) who said,

"the scholars, in the past, said: following the Sunnah is a means of salvation."

And Muwaffaq-Din Ibn Qudāmah (رَحِمَهُٱللَّه) said in the book *Rawḍā An-Nāzir*, stating the fundamentals of rulings:

"Concerning evidence, the second fundamental is the Sunnah of the Messenger of Allāh (ﷺ), what the Messenger of Allāh is considered Hujjah (evidence for or against the claimant) because the miracles attest to his sincerity, Allāh (سُبْحَانَهُوَتَعَالَى) ordered us to obey him, and warned us against opposing his commands."

Also, Al-Ḥāfiẓ Ibn Kathīr has explained the verse,

﴿ فَلْيَحْذَرِ ٱلَّذِينَ يُخَالِفُونَ عَنْ أَمْرِهِۦٓ أَن تُصِيبَهُمْ فِتْنَةٌ أَوْ يُصِيبَهُمْ عَذَابٌ أَلِيمٌ ۝ ﴾

"And let those who oppose the Messenger's (Muḥammad (صَلَّى ٱللَّهُ عَلَيْهِ وَسَلَّمَ)) commandment (i.e., his Sunnah – legal ways, orders, acts of worship, statements) (among the sects) beware, lest some Fitnah (disbelief, trials, afflictions, earthquakes, killing, overpowered by a tyrant) should befall them or a painful torment be inflicted on them." [*Sūrah an-Nūr* 24:63]

"The commandment of the Messenger of Allāh (صَلَّى ٱللَّهُ عَلَيْهِ وَسَلَّمَ) is his legal ways, methodology, Sunnah, orders and acts of worship. If one's actions and sayings agree with the actions and sayings of the Prophet (صَلَّى ٱللَّهُ عَلَيْهِ وَسَلَّمَ), it will be accepted, and if they are in opposition to it, they will be rejected."

It is related by Bukhārī and Muslim that the Messenger of Allāh (ﷺ) said,

مَنْ عَمِلَ عَمَلاً لَيْسَ عَلَيْهِ أَمْرُنَا فَهُوَ رَدٌّ

"He who does something contrary to our way (Islām) it will be rejected."

Those who do something opposing the Prophet's way essentially and seemingly some Fitnah (such as innovation, disbelief or painful torment; one may be killed or jailed) should befall on them.

Related by Imām ʾAḥmad on the authority of Abū Hurayrah (﵁) who narrated that the Messenger of Allāh (ﷺ) said,

مَثَلِي كَمَثَلِ رَجُلٍ اسْتَوْقَدَ نَارًا فَلَمَّا أَضَاءَتْ مَا حَوْلَهَا جَعَلَ الْفَرَاشُ وَهَذِهِ الدَّوَابُّ الَّتِي فِي النَّارِ يَقَعْنَ فِيهَا وَجَعَلَ يَحْجُزُهُنَّ وَيَغْلِبْنَهُ فَيَتَقَحَّمْنَ فِيهَا قَالَ فَذَلِكُمْ مَثَلِي وَمَثَلُكُمْ أَنَا آخِذٌ

بِحُجَزِكُمْ عَنِ النَّارِ هَلُمَّ عَنِ النَّارِ هَلُمَّ عَنِ النَّارِ فَتَغْلِبُونِي
تَقَحَّمُونَ فِيهَا

"My parable and that of yours is like a man who kindles a fire, and when the atmosphere was aglow, moths and insects began to fall into the fire, but I am there to hold them back, but they are plunging into it despite my efforts, and he further added: That is your example and mine. I am there to hold you back from the fire and save you from it, but you are plunging into it despite my efforts." related by 'Abdur-Razzaq.

As-Suyūtī said in a book entitled: (the key to paradise is to take Sunnah as evidence "*Miftāh Al-Jannah filihtijaj Bis-Sunnah*":

"Please, consider, may Allāh have mercy on you, that whoever rejects the matter that the narration of the Prophet (صَلَّ اللَّهُ عَلَيْهِ وَسَلَّمَ), whether is sayings or acts, as known in the fundamentals of Hadith, is evidence, he will be declared a disbeliever and left the fold of Islām, and will be resurrected with Jews and Christians, or any disbelieving sect."

Thus, there are many ahādīth and narrations related by companions and followers regarding attaching great importance to the Sunnah, the obligation of implementing it and warning against opposing it.

I hope that the verses and ahādīth we mentioned are sufficient for those who seek the truth. I beseech Allāh for all the Muslims and us to grant us success and to free us from his anger. May He guide us all to the Straight Path; He is All-Hearer, Even Near (to all things).

May Allāh raise the rank of His Servant and Messenger, our Prophet Muḥammad, his family, companions, and followers and them peace.

THE OBLIGATION OF ADHERING TO THE SUNNAH AND BEING WARY OF INNOVATION

All praise belongs to Allāh, who have perfected religion for us, and completed His Favour upon us, and have chosen Islām as our religion. May Allāh raise the rank of His Servant and Messenger who called to the obedience of Allāh and warned against extremism, innovations, and acts of disobedience. May Allāh raise his rank, his family, his companions and who follow his method and seek his guidance to the Day of Judgment and grant them peace.

To proceed:

I have read an essay in the weekly Urdu newspapers (*Idārah*) issued in the industrial city of Kanfūr, in Utter Pradesh state. The front-page states: "a propaganda campaign against the Kingdom of Saudi Arabia and being committed to the Islāmic creed, fighting innovations, and accusing the Salafi creed followed by the government is not from the Sunnah. This writer seeks to cause dissension between the people of the Sunnah (Ahlus-Sunnah) and encourage acts of innovations and superstition.

There is no doubt that this is a wicked plan and dangerous way of acting with the intent of causing harm to the Islāmic religion and spread the innovations and misguidance. This essay clearly focuses on the celebration of the Mawlid (birth) of the Messenger of Allāh (ﷺ) and consider it a reason for speaking ill against the ʿAqīdah the Kingdom and its rulership. Thus, I want to advise and warn concerning this matter. Seeking Allāh's help, I say:

It is impermissible to celebrate the Mawlid (Birth) of the Messenger of Allāh (ﷺ) or anyone else, but it is compulsory to prohibit it. It is an innovation because the Messenger of Allāh (ﷺ) did not do it or ordered anyone to do it for himself or any one of the Prophets, or his daughters, his wives or anyone of his relatives, or his companions. Also, no one of the rightly guided caliphs, the companions, the followers of faith, or anyone of the scholars did it in the preferred generations. Those know the

Sunnah best and love the Messenger of Allāh
(ﷺ) best and strictly adhered to Shariah. Had
it been a good thing, they would have preceded us
thereto.

We have been ordered to follow the Sunnah and
have been prohibited from acts of innovation. This is
because the religion of Islām is perfect, and we have
been ordered to stick to what Allāh (سُبْحَانَهُۥوَتَعَالَىٰ) and
His Messenger (ﷺ) have legislated and what
Ahlus-Sunnah, including the companions and the
followers, has approved.

It is related that the Prophet (ﷺ) said,

مَنْ أَحْدَثَ فِي أَمْرِنَا هَذَا مَا لَيْسَ مِنْهُ فَهُوَ رَدٌّ

**"He who innovates something in this matter
of ours (i.e., Islām) that is not of it will have it
rejected (by Allāh)."** Agreed upon.

In a narration by Muslim,

مَنْ عَمِلَ عَمَلاً لَيْسَ عَلَيْهِ أَمْرُنَا فَهُوَ رَدٌّ

"He who does something contrary to our way (i.e., Islām) will have it rejected."

He (ﷺ) said in another narration,

فَعَلَيْكُمْ بِسُنَّتِي وَسُنَّةِ الْخُلَفَاءِ الرّاشِدِينَ الْمَهْدِيِّينَ، عَضُّوا عَلَيْهَا بِالنَّوَاجِذِ، وَإِيَّاكُمْ وَمُحْدَثَاتِ الْأُمُورِ؛ فَإِنَّ كُلَّ بِدْعَةٍ ضَلَالَةٌ

"So, hold fast to my Sunnah and the examples of the Rightly-Guided Caliphs who will come after me. Adhere to them and hold to it fast. Beware of innovations (in Deen) because every novelty is an innovation and every innovation is an error."

These ahādīth warns us against innovations and that they are misguidance. It is also a warning of its serious danger and that the Ummah must keep away committing these acts as well as remaining distance from it. Allāh (سُبْحَانَهُ وَتَعَالَى) says,

﴿ وَمَآ ءَاتَىٰكُمُ ٱلرَّسُولُ فَخُذُوهُ وَمَا نَهَىٰكُمْ عَنْهُ فَٱنتَهُواْ ﴾

"And whatsoever the Messenger
(Muḥammad (ﷺ)) gives you, take it;
and whatsoever he forbids you, abstain (from
it)." [*Sūrah al-Hashr* 59:7]

Allāh (عَزَّوَجَلَّ) says,

$$ \text{﴿ فَلْيَحْذَرِ ٱلَّذِينَ يُخَالِفُونَ عَنْ أَمْرِهِۦٓ أَن تُصِيبَهُمْ فِتْنَةٌ أَوْ يُصِيبَهُمْ عَذَابٌ أَلِيمٌ ٦٣ ﴾} $$

"And let those who oppose the Messenger's
(Muḥammad (ﷺ)) commandment (i.e.,
his Sunnah – legal ways, orders, acts of
worship, statements) (among the sects)
beware, lest some Fitnah (disbelief, trials,
afflictions, earthquakes, killing, overpowered
by a tyrant) should befall them or a painful
torment be inflicted on them." [*Sūrah an-Nūr*
24:63]

and Allāh (سُبْحَانَهُوَتَعَالَى) says,

﴿ لَّقَدْ كَانَ لَكُمْ فِى رَسُولِ ٱللَّهِ أُسْوَةٌ حَسَنَةٌ لِّمَن كَانَ يَرْجُوا۟ ٱللَّهَ وَٱلْيَوْمَ ٱلْءَاخِرَ وَذَكَرَ ٱللَّهَ كَثِيرًا ۝ ﴾

"Indeed, in the Messenger of Allāh (Muḥammad (ﷺ)) you have a good example to follow for him who hopes for (the Meeting with) Allāh and the Last Day, and remember Allāh much." [*Sūrah al-Aḥzāb* 33:21]

and Allāh (سُبْحَانَهُ وَتَعَالَىٰ) says,

﴿ وَٱلسَّٰبِقُونَ ٱلْأَوَّلُونَ مِنَ ٱلْمُهَٰجِرِينَ وَٱلْأَنصَارِ وَٱلَّذِينَ ٱتَّبَعُوهُم بِإِحْسَٰنٍ رَّضِىَ ٱللَّهُ عَنْهُمْ وَرَضُوا۟ عَنْهُ وَأَعَدَّ لَهُمْ جَنَّٰتٍ تَجْرِى تَحْتَهَا ٱلْأَنْهَٰرُ خَٰلِدِينَ فِيهَآ أَبَدًا ذَٰلِكَ ٱلْفَوْزُ ٱلْعَظِيمُ ۝ ﴾

"And the foremost to embrace Islām of the Muhajirun (those who migrated from Makkah to Al-Madinah) and the Ansar (the citizens of Al-Madinah who helped and gave aid to the Muhajirun) and also those who followed them exactly (in Faith). Allāh is

well-pleased with them as they are well-pleased with Him. He has prepared for them Gardens under which rivers flow (Paradise), to dwell therein forever. That is the supreme success." [*Sūrah at-Tawbah* 9:100]

and Allāh (سُبْحَانَهُوَتَعَالَى) says,

﴿ ٱلْيَوْمَ أَكْمَلْتُ لَكُمْ دِينَكُمْ وَأَتْمَمْتُ عَلَيْكُمْ نِعْمَتِي وَرَضِيتُ لَكُمُ ٱلْإِسْلَٰمَ دِينًا ﴾

"This day, I have perfected your religion for you, completed My Favour upon you, and have chosen for you Islām as your religion." [*Sūrah al-Mā'idah* 5:3]

This last verse clearly indicates that Allāh (سُبْحَانَهُوَتَعَالَى) has perfected for this Ummah their religion, and completed His Favour upon them, and did not take His Prophet's life until after he conveyed the message in a plain way, and clarified the Shariah (acts and sayings).

He also stated that every act innovated by people is an innovation which should be rejected, even if his intention is good. It is clear that the Messenger of Allāh (ﷺ) and the Pious Predecessors warned against innovations because it is considered an addition to the religion. A religion which Allāh has not permitted it (innovation). This similitude and likeness are to the enemies of Allāh (Jews and Christians) who added to their religion and innovated matters Allāh has not allow. Committing an act of innovation is accusing Islām of imperfection, which is considered a great corruption and serious evil deed, and against Allāh's statement,

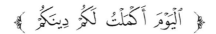

"This day, I have perfected your religion for you." [*Sūrah al-Māʾidah* 5:3]

It clearly opposes the authentic aḥādīth of the Messenger of Allāh (ﷺ) which warned against innovations.

A celebration of the Mawlid denotes that Allāh (سُبْحَانَهُوَتَعَالَى) have not perfected this religion for the Ummah and that the Messenger of Allāh (ﷺ)

did not convey the message in a clear way to be followed by the Ummah.

Though those late innovators innovated matters Allāh (سُبْحَانَهُوَتَعَالَ) has not ordained claiming that this keeps them closer to Allāh. There is no doubt that this is a great danger and opposition to Allāh (سُبْحَانَهُوَتَعَالَ) and His Messenger (صَلَّىاللَّهُعَلَيْهِوَسَلَّمَ). But Allāh (سُبْحَانَهُوَتَعَالَ) have perfected religion for them and completed His favor upon them, and the Messenger of Allāh (صَلَّىاللَّهُعَلَيْهِوَسَلَّمَ) conveyed the message in a clear way.

He (صَلَّىاللَّهُعَلَيْهِوَسَلَّمَ) has clarified for his Ummah every way which they can reach Paradise and keep them distant from Fire.

It is related in Saḥīḥ on the authority of ʿAbdullāh Ibn Amr ibn Al-Aʾs (رَضِيَاللَّهُعَنْهُمَا) that the Messenger of Allāh (صَلَّىاللَّهُعَلَيْهِوَسَلَّمَ) said,

إِنَّهُ لَمْ يَكُنْ نَبِيٌّ قَبْلِي إِلاَّ كَانَ حَقًّا عَلَيْهِ أَنْ يَدُلَّ أُمَّتَهُ عَلَى خَيْرِ مَا يَعْلَمُهُ لَهُمْ وَيُنْذِرَهُمْ شَرَّ مَا يَعْلَمُهُ لَهُمْ

"Every Prophet before me was obliged to guide his followers to what he knew was good for them and to warn the evil thing which he knew." Related by Muslim in Saḥīḥ

It is clear that our Prophet (ﷺ) is the best and last Prophet. He is best one to give advice and convey the message (of the religion), thus if celebrating the Mawlid is approved by religion, the Messenger of Allāh (ﷺ) has already clarified it for the Ummah, or his companions (رضي الله عنهم) did. But because of this occurred, Islām is against this innovation which the Messenger of Allāh (ﷺ) warned against, as mentioned in the authentic ahādīth.

Some scholars clearly denounced celebration of Mawlid and warned against it as indicated in the abovementioned ahādīth. According to the principles in the Islāmic legislation which is well-known that the source for lawful and unlawful matters, resolution for discord amongst the people are all to be referred back to the Book of Allāh and the Sunnah of the Messenger of Allāh (ﷺ) just as Allāh (سُبْحَانَهُوَتَعَالَى) says,

$$
\text{﴿ يَٰٓأَيُّهَا ٱلَّذِينَ ءَامَنُوٓاْ أَطِيعُواْ ٱللَّهَ وَأَطِيعُواْ ٱلرَّسُولَ وَأُوْلِي ٱلْأَمْرِ مِنكُمْ فَإِن تَنَٰزَعْتُمْ فِي شَيْءٍ فَرُدُّوهُ إِلَى ٱللَّهِ وَٱلرَّسُولِ إِن كُنتُمْ تُؤْمِنُونَ بِٱللَّهِ وَٱلْيَوْمِ ٱلْأَخِرِ ذَٰلِكَ خَيْرٌ وَأَحْسَنُ تَأْوِيلًا ٥٩ ﴾}
$$

"O you who believe! Obey Allāh and obey the Messenger (Muḥammad (ﷺ)), and those of you (Muslims) who are in authority. And if you differ in anything amongst yourselves, refer it to Allāh and His Messenger ((ﷺ)) if you believe in Allāh and in the Last Day. That is better and more suitable for final determination." [*Sūrah an-Nisā'* 59]

and Allāh (سُبْحَانَهُوَتَعَالَى) says,

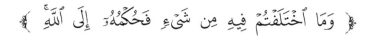

"And in whatsoever you differ, the decision thereof is with Allāh (He is the ruling Judge)."
[*Sūrah ash-Shūrā* 42:10]

If this matter (celebrating the Mawlid) is referred back to the Book of Allāh (سُبْحَانَهُوَتَعَالَ), one will find that Allāh ordered us to follow the Messenger of Allāh (صَلَّىٱللَّهُعَلَيْهِوَسَلَّمَ) and warned us against what he (صَلَّىٱللَّهُعَلَيْهِوَسَلَّمَ) has prohibited, and told us that Allāh (سُبْحَانَهُوَتَعَالَ) has perfected religion for this Ummah. Hence, the celebration of the Mawlid has not been ordered by the Messenger of Allāh (صَلَّىٱللَّهُعَلَيْهِوَسَلَّمَ). So, it is not from the religion of Islām which has been perfected by Allāh and ordered us to follow the Messenger regarding it.

If it is referred to the Sunnah of the Messenger of Allāh (صَلَّىٱللَّهُعَلَيْهِوَسَلَّمَ), no one can find that he did it or ordered anyone to do it or done by the companions (رَضِيَٱللَّهُعَنْهُمْ). Thus, it is against our religion; rather it is an innovation. It is also considered blind similitude to the people of the Book (Jews and Christians) regarding their feasts. So, it is clear for the truthful

ones that celebration of any Mawlid is against Islām
and it is an innovation which Allāh ordered us to
keep away from.

One should not be deceived by the number of people
doing this in many countries. The truth is not
declared by abundant doers but by legal evidence
just as Allāh (سُبْحَانَهُوَتَعَالَى) says about the Jews and
Christians,

﴿ وَقَالُواْ لَن يَدْخُلَ ٱلْجَنَّةَ إِلَّا مَن كَانَ هُودًا أَوْ
نَصَٰرَىٰ تِلْكَ أَمَانِيُّهُمْ قُلْ هَاتُواْ بُرْهَٰنَكُمْ إِن كُنتُمْ
صَٰدِقِينَ ﴿١١١﴾ ﴾

**"And they say, "none shall enter Paradise
unless he is a Jew or a Christian." These are
their own desires. Say (O Muḥammad
(صَلَّىاللَّهُعَلَيْهِوَسَلَّمَ)), "Produce your proof if you are
truthful." [*Sūrah al-Baqarah* 2:111]**

And Allāh (سُبْحَانَهُوَتَعَالَى) says,

﴿ وَإِن تُطِعۡ أَكۡثَرَ مَن فِى ٱلۡأَرۡضِ يُضِلُّوكَ عَن سَبِيلِ ٱللَّهِ ﴾

"And if you obey most of those on the earth; they will mislead you far away from Allāh's Path." [*Sūrah al-ʾAnʿām 7:116*]

Although most of these celebrations are innovations, it included, in many countries and many times, other evils. Such as intermingling of the sexes (men with women), songs, music, drinking alcohol and drugs and so on. There may be a greater form of Shirk in exaggerating praise of the Messenger of Allāh (ﷺ) or any Awliyā, seeking help with him, and believing that he knows unseen, and many other things make one faithless.

It is related that the Messenger of Allāh (ﷺ) said,

وَإِيَّاكُمْ وَالْغُلُوَّ فِي الدِّينِ فَإِنَّمَا أَهْلَكَ مَنْ كَانَ قَبْلَكُمُ الْغُلُوُّ فِي الدِّينِ

"Beware of going to extremes in religious matters, for those who came before you were destroyed because of going to extremes in religious matters."

Also, the Messenger of Allāh (ﷺ) said,

لَا تُطْرُونِي كَمَا أَطْرَتِ النَّصَارَى ابْنَ مَرْيَمَ، إِنَّمَا أَنَا عَبْدٌ، فَقُولُوا: عَبْدُ اللهِ وَرَسُولُهُ

"Do not exceed in praising me as the Christians over-praised Esa (that they made him the son of Allāh), I am a servant of Allāh, so call me the servant of Allāh and His Messenger." related by Bukhārī in Saḥīḥ.

It is strange that many people attend these innovated festivities and abandon Allāh's obligations including Friday prayers and congregational prayers. He does not even pay attention to this or believes that what he did is a great evil. There is no doubt that this attests to weak faith and bad insight, and that many sins and crimes cover the hearts. We beseech Allāh to give us well-being and all Muslims.

But the strangest is that they think that the Messenger of Allāh (ﷺ) attend the Mawlid, so they stand up cheering and welcoming. This is considered great ignorance and misguidance because the Messenger of Allāh (صَلَّ ٱللَّهُ عَلَيْهِ وَسَلَّمَ) will not come out of his grave before the Day of Judgment and will not contact anyone or attend their meetings, He (صَلَّ ٱللَّهُ عَلَيْهِ وَسَلَّمَ) will stay in his grave until the Day of Judgment. However, his soul is preserved in Illiyyūn in Paradise, as Allāh (سُبْحَانَهُوَتَعَالَى) says,

﴿ ثُمَّ إِنَّكُم بَعْدَ ذَٰلِكَ لَمَيِّتُونَ ۝ ثُمَّ إِنَّكُمْ يَوْمَ ٱلْقِيَٰمَةِ تُبْعَثُونَ ۝ ﴾

"After that, surely, you will die. Then (again), surely, you will be resurrected on the Day of Resurrection." [*Sūrah al-Muʾminūn* 23:15-16]

The Prophet (صَلَّ ٱللَّهُ عَلَيْهِ وَسَلَّمَ) said,

أَنَا أَوَّلُ مَنْ يَنْشَقُّ عَنْهُ الْقَبْرُ يَوْمَ الْقِيَامَةِ وَ أَنَا أَوَّلُ شَافِعٍ وَأَوَّلُ مُشَفَّعٍ

"I will be the first one for whom the earth will be split open on the Day of Resurrection. I

will be the first to intercede, and the first whose intercession will be accepted."

Both of this verse and hadith indicate that the Prophet (ﷺ) and the dead come out of their graves on the Day of Resurrection as agreed upon by the Muslim scholars. Every Muslim should pay attention to this and keep away from innovations and evils for which Allāh has sent down no authority.

Sending prayers and peace upon the Messenger of Allāh (ﷺ) is one of the best acts of worship as Allāh (سُبْحَانَهُوَتَعَالَى) says,

$$ ﴿ إِنَّ ٱللَّهَ وَمَلَٰٓئِكَتَهُۥ يُصَلُّونَ عَلَى ٱلنَّبِيِّ يَٰٓأَيُّهَا ٱلَّذِينَ ءَامَنُوا۟ صَلُّوا۟ عَلَيْهِ وَسَلِّمُوا۟ تَسْلِيمًا ۝ ﴾ $$

"Allāh sends His Salat (Graces, Honors, Blessings, Mercy) on the Prophet (Muḥammad (ﷺ)), and also His angels (ask Allāh to bless and forgive him). O you who believe! Send your Salat on (ask Allāh to bless) him (Muḥammad (ﷺ)), and (you

should) greet (salute) him with the Islāmic way of greeting (salutation, i.e., **As-Salam Alaykum**)." [*Sūrah al-Aḥzāb* 33:56]

And the Prophet (ﷺ) said,

مَنْ صَلَّى عَلَيَّ وَاحِدَةً صَلَّى اللهُ عَلَيْهِ عَشْرًا

"Whoever sends Salah upon me once, Allāh (سُبْحَانَهُوَتَعَالَى) will send Salah upon tenfold"

It is permissible at all times and stressed supererogation, but many scholars believe it to be obligatory in the last Tashahhud of every prayer, and stressed supererogation in many times, such as after announcement of prayers, during the legislated remembrance performed by the Prophet (ﷺ), in day and night of Friday as indicated in many aḥādīth. This is what I want to say about this matter; I think it is sufficient for those who are truthful.

It is strange that these innovated celebrations committed by Muslims who have a firm belief and love the Messenger of Allāh (ﷺ). We say if you were Sunni and following the Messenger of Allāh (ﷺ), did the Prophet (ﷺ), or any of his companions or his followers celebrate the Mawlid? Rather it is only the blind similitude of the enemies of Islām (Jews and Christians) and so on.

Love of the Messenger of Allāh (ﷺ) is not expressed by making feasts of the Mawlid, but by obeying his orders, believing in what he tells, abstaining from what he has forbidden, and only worship Allāh according to his Sunnah.

Also, this love is expressed by sending prayers upon him upon mentioning him, in prayers, and at any suitable time. Wahhabi, according to him, is not the only one who denounced these innovated matters. But the Wahhabi creed means sticking to the Book of Allāh and the Sunnah of the Messenger of Allāh (ﷺ) and following his way, and the way of rightly guided caliphs and the followers, and the way of the righteous Salaf, and the Imāms of religion, the people of fiqh and Fatwa regarding knowing Allāh, stating the Names and Attributes of Allāh which are mentioned in the Noble Qur'ān, and stated by the authentic ahādīth, and accepted by the companions of the Messenger of Allāh (ﷺ),

they affirm Allāh with these names and believe in them without changing their meaning or ignoring them completely or twisting the meanings or likening them to any of the created things. They stick to what the followers of the companions believe in, and the righteous Salaf, the people of faith, knowledge, and piety.

They believe that the fundamental of 'Īmān (faith) is to testify that none has the right to be worshipped but Allāh and Muḥammad is the Messenger of Allāh; it is the fundamental belief in Allāh only, it is the best branches of faith.

They know that this fundamental is based on knowledge, practicing and belief, as agreed by scholars. It indicates the obligation of worshipping Allāh Alone, no partners with Him, and to free oneself from worshipping others with Him, whomever it may by.

This is the wisdom behind Allāh creating the Jinn and mankind, and for which Messengers have been sent, and Books have been sent down.

It indicates fully love and being humble to Allāh Alone, it includes full obedience and attaching great importance to it. It indicates that only the religion of Islām is accepted by Allāh. No other religion is accepted by the earlier and later generations. The Prophets followed this religion of Islām, and they were sent for the purpose of calling to Islām and submitting to Allāh Alone.

Thus, whoever submits to Him and others, or calls Him and others is declared to be a polytheist, and whoever does not submit to Him is declared to be obstinate from worshipping Him. Allāh (سُبْحَانَهُوَتَعَالَى) says

$$ ﴿ وَلَقَدْ بَعَثْنَا فِى كُلِّ أُمَّةٍ رَّسُولًا أَنِ اعْبُدُواْ اللَّهَ وَاجْتَنِبُواْ الطَّغُوتَ ﴾ $$

"And verily, We have sent among every Ummah (community, nation) a Messenger (proclaiming): "Worship Allāh (Alone), and avoid (or keep away from) Tāghūt (all false deities, i.e., do not worship Tāghūt besides Allāh)." [*Sūrah an-Nahl* 16:36]

Their creed is based on actualizing the testimony that Muḥammad is the Messenger of Allāh, discarding innovations and every act against the Sunnah of Muḥammad, the Messenger of Allāh (ﷺ). This is the creed and Da'wah of Shaykh Muḥammad Ibn 'Abdul-Wahhāb (رحمه الله). Whoever attributed to him any other creed, they have lied.

Allāh (سبحانه وتعالى) will punish them because of these lies against him. He (رحمه الله) made fruitful essays, good treatises and great writings on the subject of 'Imān, Tawḥīd, and the testimony that none has the right to be worshipped but Allāh. All of which is stated by the Book, the Sunnah and unanimity (Ijma') including that none has the right to be worshipped but Allāh Alone.

It is clear for anyone who knows the writings of the Shaykh and his famous call, and what distinguishes his noble followers and students must know that he followed the righteous Salaf and the rightly guided Imams including worshipping Allāh Alone and keeping innovations away.

This what the rule of Saudi Arabia is based on, and the scholars take the same way; all praise belongs to

Allāh. The Saudi government is strictly against innovations and over-praise of the Messenger of Allāh (ﷺ). In Saudi Arabia, the scholars, Muslims, and rulers respect and appreciate every Muslim from any country. They only denounce those of astray creeds and the innovations and innovated feasts they did which Allāh and His Messenger have not ordained. This is prohibited because it is a novelty and every novelty is an innovation.

The Muslims have been ordered to adhere and not innovate in the religion of Islām due to its perfection and what Allāh and His Messenger legislated is sufficient; and that Ahlu Sunnah wal Jama'ah accepts this and learns it from the Companions and those who follow them and their way in excellence.

Preventing the performance of the innovated celebration of the Mawlid of the Messenger of Allāh (ﷺ) and what it entails of over-praise of the Prophet (ﷺ) and Shirk is not a degradation of the Messenger of Allāh (ﷺ). Rather it is an act of obedience to him, and compliance to his commands whereas he (صَلَّى ٱللَّهُ عَلَيْهِ وَسَلَّمَ) said,

وَإِيَّاكُمْ وَالْغُلُوَّ فِي الدِّينِ فَإِنَّمَا أَهْلَكَ مَنْ كَانَ قَبْلَكُمُ الْغُلُوُّ فِي الدِّينِ

"Beware of going to extremes in religious matters, for those who came before you were destroyed because of going to extremes in religious matters."

And he (صَلَّى ٱللَّهُ عَلَيْهِ وَسَلَّمَ) also said,

لَا تُطْرُونِي كَمَا أَطْرَتِ النَّصَارَى ابْنَ مَرْيَمَ، إِنَّمَا أَنَا عَبْدٌ، فَقُولُوا: عَبْدُ اللهِ وَرَسُولُهُ

"Do not exceed in praising me as the Christians over-praised Esa (that they made him the son of Allāh). I am the servant of Allāh. Therefore, call me the servant of Allāh and His Messenger."

This is what I want to advise to in the above-mentioned essay. May Allāh grant us success and all Muslim to understand religion and to hold fast to it. May Allāh bestow upon us sticking to the Sunnah and be wary of innovation. He is Most Beneficial and Most Generous. May Allāh raise the rank of our Prophet, Muḥammad, his family and his companions and grant them peace.

General President for scholarly research, Iftā and Da'wah, and Guidance

Abdul-Azīz Ibn ʿAbdullāh Ibn Bāz

APPENDIX 1: THE OBLIGATION OF ADHERING TO THE QURʾĀN AND THE SUNNAH AND THE PROHIBITION OF ACTS OF INNOVATION IN THE MONTH OF SHʿABĀN AS WELL AS ANY OTHER MONTH [3]

FIRST KHUTBAH

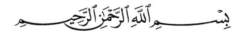

All praise belongs to Allāh, the Lord, and Master of all that exists. He is the One who ordered us to follow the Qurʾān and the Sunnah. He prohibited us from acts of innovation and causing fitnah. I openly testify that none has the right to be worshipped in truth except Allāh alone who has no partners.

---

[3] **TN:** This sermon is from Shaykh Ṣāliḥ Fawzān al-Fawzān

Whoever obeys Allāh and His Messenger has been guided and whoever disobeys them as definitely gone astray in which he only brings harm to himself and doesn't harm Allāh in the least.

I also openly testify that Muḥammad is Allāh's servant and Messenger who left his Ummah upon clarity in which only those who deviate from it will be ruined. May Allāh raise his rank and grant him, his family, and all of his companions who followed his methodology and clung to his Sunnah peace.

To proceed:

O, people! Have Taqwā of Allāh (سُبْحَانَهُوَتَعَالَى) and cling to His Book and the Sunnah of His Prophet. For indeed, within clinging to them is sufficient, guidance, and light. O, people! Beware of newly invented matters for indeed they are forms of misguidance and deception. Allāh (سُبْحَانَهُوَتَعَالَى) says,

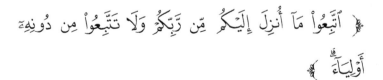

﴿ ٱتَّبِعُواْ مَآ أُنزِلَ إِلَيْكُم مِّن رَّبِّكُمْ وَلَا تَتَّبِعُواْ مِن دُونِهِۦٓ أَوْلِيَآءَ ﴾

"Follow what has been sent down unto you from your Lord (the Qur'an and Prophet Muhammad's *Sunnah*), and follow not any *Awliyā'* (protectors and helpers, etc. who order you to associate partners in worship with Allāh), besides Him (Allāh)." [*Sūrah al-ʿArāf* 7:3]

Allāh (سُبْحَانَهُوَتَعَالَى) also said,

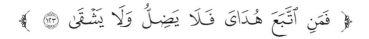

﴾ فَمَنِ ٱتَّبَعَ هُدَاىَ فَلَا يَضِلُّ وَلَا يَشْقَىٰ ۝ ﴿

"then whoever follows My Guidance shall neither go astray nor fall into distress and misery." [*Sūrah Taha* 20:123]

Indeed, Allāh has promised that whoever adheres to His Book (Qurʾān) and implements it will not be misled in this worldly life nor will he be wretched in the hereafter. He has also threatened whoever rejects His Book. Allāh (سُبْحَانَهُوَتَعَالَى) says,

﴾ وَمَنْ أَعْرَضَ عَن ذِكْرِى فَإِنَّ لَهُۥ مَعِيشَةً ضَنكًا وَنَحْشُرُهُۥ يَوْمَ ٱلْقِيَٰمَةِ أَعْمَىٰ ۝ ﴿

"But whosoever turns away from My Reminder (i.e., neither believes in this Qur'an nor acts on its orders, etc.) verily, for him is a life of hardship, and We shall raise him up blind on the Day of Resurrection." [*Sūrah Taha* 20:124]

So, whoever goes against Allāh command and what He has revealed to His Messenger and rejects it will be forgotten, and takes his guidance from other than that will have happened to him as Allāh (سُبْحَانَهُ وَتَعَالَى) says,

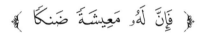

"verily, for him is a life of hardship."

Meaning, he will have a life of difficulty without any tranquility and happiness. Rather, his heart will feel constricted because of his misguidance. Even if he outwardly appears happy and he wears whatever he wants, eats whatever he wants, indeed his heart is in unrest, confusion, and uncertainty.

Some other scholars have said concerning this verse,

"Indeed, the life of hardship mentioned in this verse refers to the one's grave as it tightens on him to the point his ribs are crushed together."

The statement where Allāh (سُبْحَانَهُوَتَعَالَى) says,

"and We shall raise him up blind on the Day of Resurrection."

Refers to him being blind physically as well as in knowledge just as Allāh (سُبْحَانَهُوَتَعَالَى) said in another verse,

﴿ وَنَحۡشُرُهُمۡ يَوۡمَ ٱلۡقِيَٰمَةِ عَلَىٰ وُجُوهِهِمۡ عُمۡيٗا وَبُكۡمٗا وَصُمّٗا مَّأۡوَىٰهُمۡ جَهَنَّمُ ﴾

"and We shall gather them together on the Day of Resurrection on their faces, blind, dumb and deaf, their abode will be Hell." [*Sūrah al-Israa* 17:97]

Allāh has ordered obedience to Him and His Messenger in numerous verses, and obedience to Allāh is by adhering to His Book and obedience to the Messenger is by adhering to His Sunnah. Allāh (سُبْحَانَهُوَتَعَالَى) says,

﴿ تِلْكَ حُدُودُ ٱللَّهِ وَمَن يُطِعِ ٱللَّهَ وَرَسُولَهُ يُدْخِلْهُ جَنَّٰتٍ تَجْرِى مِن تَحْتِهَا ٱلْأَنْهَٰرُ خَٰلِدِينَ فِيهَا وَذَٰلِكَ ٱلْفَوْزُ ٱلْعَظِيمُ ۞ وَمَن يَعْصِ ٱللَّهَ وَرَسُولَهُ وَيَتَعَدَّ حُدُودَهُ يُدْخِلْهُ نَارًا خَٰلِدًا فِيهَا وَلَهُ عَذَابٌ مُّهِينٌ ۞ ﴾

"And whosoever obeys Allāh and His Messenger (Muḥammad ﷺ) will be admitted to Gardens under which rivers flow (in Paradise), to abide therein, and that will be the great success. And whosoever disobeys Allāh and His Messenger (Muḥammad ﷺ) and transgresses His limits, He will cast him into the Fire, to abide therein; and he shall have a disgraceful torment." [*Sūrah an-Nisā'* 4:13-14]

This is from the requisites of testifying that none has the right to be worshipped in truth except Allāh alone and that Muḥammad is the Messenger of Allāh. So, whoever testifies that none has the right to be worshipped, in truth, except Allāh alone, he becomes duty-bound to obey Allāh and adhere to His Book. Likewise, whoever testifies that Muḥammad is the Messenger of Allāh is duty bound to obey him and adhere to His Sunnah.

Allāh (سُبْحَانَهُوَتَعَالَى) has informed us that whoever obeys the Messenger (صَلَّىٰاللَّهُعَلَيْهِوَسَلَّمَ) has demonstrated proof of his love for Allāh as well as Allāh's love for his servant. On the other hand, whoever doesn't obey the Messenger has furnished proof of his disbelief. Allāh (سُبْحَانَهُوَتَعَالَى) says,

$$﴿ قُلْ إِن كُنتُمْ تُحِبُّونَ ٱللَّهَ فَٱتَّبِعُونِي يُحْبِبْكُمُ ٱللَّهُ وَيَغْفِرْ لَكُمْ ذُنُوبَكُمْ وَٱللَّهُ غَفُورٌ رَّحِيمٌ ۝ قُلْ أَطِيعُوا۟ ٱللَّهَ وَٱلرَّسُولَ فَإِن تَوَلَّوْا۟ فَإِنَّ ٱللَّهَ لَا يُحِبُّ ٱلْكَٰفِرِينَ ۝ ﴾$$

"Say (O Muḥammad صَلَّىٰاللَّهُعَلَيْهِوَسَلَّمَ to mankind): "If you (really) love Allāh then follow me (i.e., accept Islāmic Monotheism, follow the

Qur'ān and the *Sunnah*), Allāh will love you and forgive you of your sins. And Allāh is Oft-Forgiving, Most Merciful." Say (O Muḥammad ﷺ): "Obey Allāh and the Messenger (Muḥammad ﷺ)." But if they turn away, then Allāh does not like the disbelievers." [*Sūrah 'Ali 'Imrān* 3:31-32]

Allāh (سُبْحَانَهُوَتَعَالَى) has informed us that whoever has obeyed the Messenger has surely Allāh obeyed. This is because obedience to the Messenger is obedience to the one who sent him (i.e., the Messenger). Allāh (سُبْحَانَهُوَتَعَالَى) says,

﴿ مَّن يُطِعِ ٱلرَّسُولَ فَقَدْ أَطَاعَ ٱللَّهَ ﴾

"He who obeys the Messenger (Muḥammad ﷺ), has indeed obeyed Allāh." [*Sūrah an-Nisā'* 4:80]

Allāh (سُبْحَانَهُوَتَعَالَى) informed us that whoever obeys the Messenger (ﷺ) has obtained complete guidance. Allāh (سُبْحَانَهُوَتَعَالَى) says,

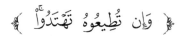

﴿ وَإِن تُطِيعُوهُ تَهْتَدُواْ ﴾

"If you obey him, you shall be on the right guidance." [*Sūrah an-Nūr* 24:54]

Allāh (سُبْحَانَهُوَتَعَالَى) has informed us also that obedience to the Messenger is a cause and means for mercy. Allāh (سُبْحَانَهُوَتَعَالَى) says,

﴿ وَأَطِيعُواْ ٱللَّهَ وَٱلرَّسُولَ لَعَلَّكُمْ تُرْحَمُونَ ۞ ﴾

"And obey Allāh and the Messenger (Muḥammad صَلَّىٱللَّهُعَلَيْهِوَسَلَّمَ) that you may obtain mercy." [*Sūrah 'Āli Imran* 3:132]

Allāh has informed us that whoever disobeys the Messenger (صَلَّىٱللَّهُعَلَيْهِوَسَلَّمَ) is misguided and follows his wimps and desires. Allāh (سُبْحَانَهُوَتَعَالَى) says,

﴿ فَإِن لَّمْ يَسْتَجِيبُواْ لَكَ فَٱعْلَمْ أَنَّمَا يَتَّبِعُونَ أَهْوَآءَهُمْ وَمَنْ أَضَلُّ مِمَّنِ ٱتَّبَعَ هَوَٰهُ بِغَيْرِ هُدًى مِّنَ ٱللَّهِ ﴾

"But if they answer you not (i.e., do not believe in your doctrine of Islamic Monotheism, nor follow you), then know that they only follow their own lusts. And who is more astray than one who follows his own

lusts, without guidance from Allāh?" [*Sūrah al-Qasas* 28:50]

Allāh has threatened whoever goes against the Messenger's commands with torment in this life as well as the hereafter. Allāh (سُبْحَانَهُوَتَعَالَى) says,

﴿ لِوَاذًا فَلْيَحْذَرِ ٱلَّذِينَ يُخَالِفُونَ عَنْ أَمْرِهِۦٓ أَن تُصِيبَهُمْ فِتْنَةٌ أَوْ يُصِيبَهُمْ عَذَابٌ أَلِيمٌ ٦٣ ﴾

"under shelter. And let those who oppose the Messenger's (Muḥammad صَلَّىٱللَّهُعَلَيْهِوَسَلَّمَ) commandment (i.e., his *Sunnah legal ways, orders, acts of worship, statements, etc.*) (*among the sects*) beware, lest some Fitnah (disbelief, trials, afflictions, earthquakes, killing, overpowered by a tyrant, etc.) befall them or a painful torment be inflicted on them." [*Sūrah an-Nūr* 24:63]

Ibn Kathīr (رَحِمَهُٱللَّه) commenting on the previous verse said,

"Whoever opposes the Messenger (صَلَّىٱللَّهُعَلَيْهِوَسَلَّمَ) outwardly and inwardly should beware and be afraid, **"lest some fitnah befall them"** of disbelief, hypocrisy, or innovation in their hearts, **"or a painful torment be inflicted on them"** in this worldly life by way of murder, capital punishment, imprisonment, or the like thereof."

The Prophet (ﷺ) use to warn against opposing the Qurʾān and the Sunnah. He also clarified that whatever opposes the Qurʾān and the Sunnah is an act of innovation and misguidance. The Prophet (ﷺ) would say in his sermons,

فَإِنَّ خَيْرَ الْحَدِيثِ كِتَابُ اللهِ وَخَيْرُ الْهُدَى هُدَى مُحَمَّدٍ وَشَرُّ الأُمُورِ مُحْدَثَاتُهَا وَكُلُّ بِدْعَةٍ ضَلاَلَةٌ

"The best of the speech is embodied in the Book of Allāh, and the best of the guidance is the guidance given by Muḥammad. And the evilest affairs are their innovations, and every innovation is a misguidance."

He (ﷺ) also said,

فَإِنَّهُ مَنْ يَعِشْ مِنْكُمْ فَسَيَرَى اخْتِلَافًا كَثِيرًا، فَعَلَيْكُمْ بِسُنَّتِي وَسُنَّةِ الْخُلَفَاءِ الرَّاشِدِينَ الْمَهْدِيِينَ، عَضُّوا عَلَيْهَا بِالنَّوَاجِذِ، وَإِيَّاكُمْ وَمُحْدَثَاتِ الْأُمُورِ؛ فَإِنَّ كُلَّ بِدْعَةٍ ضَلَالَةٌ

"Verily he among you who lives long will see great controversy, so you must keep to my Sunnah and to the Sunnah of the Khulafa ar-Rashideen (the rightly guided caliphs), those who guide to the right way. Cling to it stubbornly [literally: with your molar teeth]. Beware of newly invented matters [in the religion], for verily every Bid'ah (innovation) is misguidance."

Al-Bukhārī and Muslim reported that the Prophet (صَلَّى اللَّهُ عَلَيْهِ وَسَلَّمَ) said,

مَنْ أَحْدَثَ فِي أَمْرِنَا هَذَا مَا لَيْسَ مِنْهُ فَهُوَ رَدٌّ

"He who innovates something in this matter of ours (i.e., Islam) that is not of it will have it rejected (by Allāh)."

And in another version (of the previous Ḥadīth) reported by Imām Muslim, the Prophet (ﷺ) said,

مَنْ عَمِلَ عَمَلًا لَيْسَ عَلَيْهِ أَمْرُنَا فَهُوَ رَدٌّ

"He who does an act which we have not commanded will have it rejected (by Allāh)."

Meaning, the one who introduced a newly invented matter or innovation will not be accepted. This is because the action is in opposition to what Allāh has legislated for His servants.

These textual evidences and the like thereof contain a warning against acts of innovation and oppositions. Acts of innovation are newly invented paths in the religion of Islām which have no evidence from the Qurʾān and the Sunnah. The person who does this intends to gain nearness to Allāh (ﻋﺰﻭﺟﻞ) by way of those actions. It comes in numerous forms like:

❖ introducing an act of worship which Allāh or His Messenger did not legislate,

❖ specifying a particular time for worship which Allāh or His Messenger have not specified,

❖ or performing an act of worship in a certain matter which Allāh and His Messenger have not legislated.

It is possible that innovation can come in the form introducing an act of worship which has no basis in the legislation of Islām similar to the innovation of celebrating the birth of the Prophet (صَلَّى اللهُ عَلَيْهِ وَسَلَّمَ), the Prophet's ascending and descending from heaven, or the Prophet's migration.

It is also possible that innovation can come in the form of specifying a particular time for worship which is found in the legislation like the performing acts of worship like Ṣalāh, legislative remembrances of Allāh, and supplication in the month of Rajab and/or the 15th night of Shʿabān. Also, like specifically seeking out the 15th day of Shʿabān for fasting.

It is possible that innovation can come in the form of worship being performed in particular manner which has not been legislated. Like performing supplication in congregation after one of the five daily prayers or performing legislative remembrances in congregation and the like thereof.

Acts of innovation deter one from the religion of Allāh, obtaining nearness to Allāh, and brings about chastisement in this life as well as the hereafter; that is because acts of innovation are from the religion of Shayṭān not the religion of Ar-Rahmān (the Most Merciful).

The innovator is he who follows his wimps and desires as Allāh (سُبْحَانَهُوَتَعَالَى) mentions,

﴿ وَمَنْ أَضَلُّ مِمَّنِ ٱتَّبَعَ هَوَىٰهُ بِغَيْرِ هُدًى مِّنَ ٱللَّهِ ﴾

"And who is more astray than one who follows his own lusts, without guidance from Allāh?" [*Sūrah al-Qasas* 28:50]

The innovator speaks about Allāh without knowledge; and speaking about Allāh without knowledge is connected to Shirk in which Allāh cautions from in the following verse,

﴿ قُل إِنَّمَا حَرَّمَ رَبِّيَ ٱلْفَوَٰحِشَ مَا ظَهَرَ مِنْهَا وَمَا بَطَنَ وَٱلْإِثْمَ وَٱلْبَغْىَ بِغَيْرِ ٱلْحَقِّ وَأَن تُشْرِكُوا۟ بِٱللَّهِ مَا لَمْ يُنَزِّلْ بِهِۦ سُلْطَٰنًا وَأَن تَقُولُوا۟ عَلَى ٱللَّهِ مَا لَا تَعْلَمُونَ ٣٣ ﴾

"Say (O Muḥammad ﷺ): "(But) the things that my Lord has indeed forbidden are *Al-Fawāhish* (great evil sins, every kind of unlawful sexual intercourse, etc.) whether committed openly or secretly, sins (of all kinds), unrighteous oppression, joining partners (in worship) with Allāh for which He has given no authority, and saying things about Allāh of which you have no knowledge." [*Sūrah al-'Arāf* 7:33]

Al-Imām Ibn al-Qayyim (رَحِمَهُ ٱللَّهُ) said about this,

"Speaking about Allāh without knowledge and Shirk are inseparable. When this misguided act of innovation is a form of ignorance concerning Allāh's attributes and a denial of what we have been informed about Allāh from Himself and His messenger (ﷺ) this becomes greatest major sin even if it is limited to disbelief; it is also more beloved to Iblees than acts of disobedience. This is because one seeks repentance from acts of disobedience, yet one doesn't seek repentance from acts of innovation. Iblees — may Allāh curse him — said, "I have ruined the children of ʾĀdam with sin, and they have ruined me with the statement of Tawhīd (Lā ilāh illallāh) and seeking forgiveness. So, when I became aware of that I propagated among them lower desires, and they started committing sins (innovations) not seeking repentance from it. Because to them, they were doing righteous deeds."

It is well-known that the one who commits sin only causes harm to himself. However, the innovator brings harm to the people. So, the fitnah of the innovator is caused by the foundation of one's religion whereas the fitnah of the sinner is caused by his lower desires.

The innovator alleges that His Lord hasn't completed His religion before the passing away of the Prophet (صَلَّى ٱللَّهُ عَلَيْهِ وَسَلَّمَ). So essentially this individual has rejected Allāh's (سُبْحَانَهُ وَتَعَالَىٰ) statement,

﴿ ٱلْيَوْمَ أَكْمَلْتُ لَكُمْ دِينَكُمْ ﴾

"This day, I have perfected your religion for you." [*Sūrah al-Mā'idah* 5:3]

Or one questions that the Messenger didn't convey the message. In reality, the innovator only wants to split the ranks of the Muslims. Because the unity of the Muslims only actualizes adherence to what Allāh has legislated just as He (سُبْحَانَهُ وَتَعَالَى) says,

﴿ وَٱعْتَصِمُوا بِحَبْلِ ٱللَّهِ جَمِيعًا وَلَا تَفَرَّقُوا ﴾

"And hold fast, all of you together, to the Rope of Allāh (i.e., this Qur'an), and be not divided among yourselves" [*Sūrah 'Āli 'Imrān* 3:102]

And Allāh (سُبْحَانَهُ وَتَعَالَى) says,

﴿ وَأَنَّ هَٰذَا صِرَٰطِي مُسْتَقِيمًا فَٱتَّبِعُوهُ وَلَا تَتَّبِعُوا ٱلسُّبُلَ فَتَفَرَّقَ بِكُمْ عَن سَبِيلِهِ ﴾

"And verily, this (i.e., Allāh's Commandments mentioned in the above two Verses 151 and 152) is my Straight Path, so follow it, and follow not (other) paths, for they will separate you away from His Path." [*Sūrah al-ʾAnʿām* 6:153]

So, the innovator wants to separate the Muslims from Allāh's straight path. He wants to turn them away from Allāh's path of monotheism to the various paths of innovation. Because acts of innovation don't stop at its limit nor doesn't it conclude at its objective. Every innovator has he own specific path, unlike another innovator. The Prophet (ﷺ) illustrated that when he drew a line in the sand,

هَذَا سَبِيلُ اللهِ مُسْتَقِيماً ، وَ خَطَّ خُطُوطاً عَنْ يَمِينِهِ وَ شِمَالِهِ ثُمَّ قَالَ : هَذِهِ السُّبُلُ لَيْسَ مِنْهَا سَبِيلٌ إِلَّا عَلَيْهِ شَيْطَانٌ يَدْعُو إِلَيْهِ ثُمَّ قَرَأَ : ﴿ وَأَنَّ هَذَا صِرَاطِى مُسْتَقِيمًا فَاتَّبِعُوهُ وَلَا تَتَّبِعُواْ السُّبُلَ فَتَفَرَّقَ بِكُمْ عَن سَبِيلِهِ ﴾

"This is the straight path of Allāh. Then he drew several lines to the right and left of it

and said, 'these lines only have a Shayṭān at the end of it calling to it.' Then he recited, "And verily, this (i.e., Allāh's Commandments mentioned in the above two Verses 151 and 152) is my Straight Path, so follow it, and follow not (other) paths, for they will separate you away from His Path.""
Imām ʾAḥmad and al-Haakim reported it.

This Ḥadīth proves that acts of innovation only separate and splits the Muslims.

O servants of Allāh! Indeed, we are living in a time where innovations are abundantly increasing, and the innovators are active. They are circulating innovations amongst the people as well as propagating it at every opportunity. This is because of the correct religion's strangeness to the people and the rarity of scholars who rectify the masses.

Among these innovations that are circulated every year and misled the ignorant and laymen is the celebration on the 15th night of Shʿabān in which it specified for various types of legislated remembrances and Ṣalāh. This is because they allege that this night is when the appointed times, provisions, and what occurs in the following year are decreed. They allege that this night should be taken interest to because of Allāh's statement,

"Therein (that night) is decreed every matter of ordainments." [*Sūrah ad-Dukhān* 44:4]

They single out the fifteenth of Shʿabān for fasting acting in according to a Ḥadīth pertaining to this subject all of which is an innovation. Because there is nothing — Ḥadīth wise-- that establishes singling out the fifteenth night of Shʿabān for legislated remembrances, night prayer, or fasting during that day. As long as there is not a single established proof for it, then it is an act of innovation in the religion and opposition to the Muslims who cling to the Sunnah and leave off innovation.

There are some scholars who have statements regarding this night. Abū Bakr Muḥammad bin al-Walīd at-Tartūshī who mentioned in his book *Newly invented matters and innovations*,

"Ibn Waḍāh reported on the authority of Zayd ibn Aslām who said, 'We do not know any of our scholars and jurists who take into consideration the 15th night of Sh'abān (for worship) nor do they deem it to have virtue over the other days."

Ibn Rajab (رَحِمَهُ ٱللَّهُ) mentioned in his book *Lataaif al-Maarif*,

"Singling out the fifteenth night of Sh'abān is rejected by many of the scholars of the Arabian Peninsula. Among them are Ataa and Ibn Abū Maleekah. 'Abdur Rahmaan bin Zayd bin Aslām reported from the jurists of al-Madīnah which is a statement of the Maliki scholars and others who stated, 'This is an act of innovation' they also stated, 'there is nothing affirmed from the Prophet (صَلَّىٱللَّهُعَلَيْهِوَسَلَّمَ) or his Companions for singling out the fifteenth night of Sh'abān to perform the night prayer."

Al-Ḥāfiẓ al-'Irāqī (رَحِمَهُ ٱللَّهُ) stated also,

"The Ḥadīth on performing the night prayer on the fifteenth night of Sh'abān is false."

As for performing the fast on the fifteenth day of Shʿabān, there is not a single Ḥadīth from the Prophet (ﷺ) affirmed so. However, there is a Ḥadīth mentioned on the subject, yet it is Daeef (weak) just as Ibn Rajab and others have cited; and weak narrations are not to be used to establish proof (in the religion).

As for those who allege that the fifteenth night of Shʿabān is the night of Decree in which the deeds for the following year are sent down, and they use a proof Allāh's (سُبْحَانَهُ وَتَعَالَى) statement,

$$\text{﴿ إِنَّا أَنزَلْنَٰهُ فِى لَيْلَةٍ مُّبَٰرَكَةٍ إِنَّا كُنَّا مُنذِرِينَ ۝ فِيهَا يُفْرَقُ كُلُّ أَمْرٍ حَكِيمٍ ۝ ﴾}$$

"We sent it (this Qur'an) down on a blessed night [(i.e., the night of *Qadr*, *Sūrah* No: 97) in the month of Ramaḍān, the 9th month of the Islamic calendar]. Verily, We are ever warning [mankind that Our Torment will reach those who disbelieve in Our Oneness of Lordship and in Our Oneness of worship]. Therein (that night) is decreed every matter of ordainments." [*Sūrah ad-Dukhān* 44:3-4]

Their using this verse as proof is false and baseless as what is really intended by "night" is the night of Decree as Allāh mentions in another verse,

$$ \{ \; \textcolor{black}{إِنَّآ أَنزَلۡنَٰهُ فِى لَيۡلَةِ ٱلۡقَدۡرِ} \; ① \; \} $$

"Verily! We have sent it (this Qur'an) down in the night of *Al-Qadr* (Decree)." [*Sūrah al-Qadr* 97:1]

Which is in the month Ramaḍān not Shʿabān just as Allāh (سُبۡحَانَهُۥوَتَعَالَىٰ) says,

$$ \{ \; \textcolor{black}{شَهۡرُ رَمَضَانَ ٱلَّذِىٓ أُنزِلَ فِيهِ ٱلۡقُرۡءَانُ} \; \} $$

"The month of Ramaḍān in which was revealed the Qurʾān." [*Sūrah al-Baqarah* 2:185]

Thus, the Qurʾān sent down on the night of Qadr undoubtedly in the month of Ramaḍān, and the proof was the previously cited verse (Sūrah al-Baqarah 2:185).

Ibn Kathīr (رَحِمَهُٱللَّه) said regarding this matter,

"Allāh (رَحِمَهُٱللَّه) informs us about the Great Qurʾān was revealed on a blessed night, and this is the night of Qadr as He (عَزَّوَجَلَّ) mentions,

$$ \text{﴿ إِنَّآ أَنزَلۡنَٰهُ فِى لَيۡلَةِ ٱلۡقَدۡرِ ۝ ﴾} $$

"Verily! We have sent it (this Qur'an) down in the night of Al-Qadr (Decree)." [*Sūrah al-Qadr* 97:1]

Which is in the month of Ramaḍān as Allāh (سُبۡحَانَهُۥوَتَعَالَىٰ) says in another verse,

$$ \text{﴿ شَهۡرُ رَمَضَانَ ٱلَّذِىٓ أُنزِلَ فِيهِ ٱلۡقُرۡءَانُ ﴾} $$

"The month of Ramaḍān in which was revealed the Qurʾān." [*Sūrah al-Baqarah* 2:185]

So, whoever says that is on the fifteenth night of Shʿabān as reported by Ikrimah is highly mistaken and misguided. As for the Ḥadīth reported concerning the fifteenth night of Shʿabān in which the Prophet (صَلَّىٱللَّهُعَلَيۡهِوَسَلَّمَ) said,

"the appointed terms from one Shʿabān to the next have been cut off even so much that a man marries, is born, and his name is among the dead."

Is a Ḥadīth *Mursal*[4]."

In closing — O servants of Allāh! Have Taqwā of Allāh, cling to the Book of your Lord and the Sunnah of your Prophet as well as what the Pious Predecessor was upon. Be wary of acts of innovation and those who propagate it just the Prophet (ﷺ) warned us about.

I seek refuge with Allāh from the accursed Shayṭān. In the name of Allāh, the Most Merciful, the Bestower of vast Mercy (to the believers),

$$﴿ وَأَنَّ هَـٰذَا صِرَٰطِى مُسْتَقِيمًا فَٱتَّبِعُوهُ وَلَا تَتَّبِعُوا۟ ٱلسُّبُلَ فَتَفَرَّقَ بِكُمْ عَن سَبِيلِهِۦ ذَٰلِكُمْ وَصَّىٰكُم بِهِۦ لَعَلَّكُمْ تَتَّقُونَ ۝ ﴾$$

---

[4] **TN:** Ḥadīth *Mursal* is a reported by a Tābiʿ (second generation Muslim) omitting the mentioning a Companion of the Prophet. It is deemed to be weak narration and not to be taken.

"And verily, this (i.e., Allāh's Commandments mentioned in the above two Verses 151 and 152) is my Straight Path, so follow it, and follow not (other) paths, for they will separate you away from His Path. This He has ordained for you that you may become *Al-Muttaqūn* (the pious - see V.2:2)." [*Sūrah al-ʾAnʿām 6:154*]

SECOND KHUTBAH

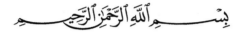

All praise belongs to Allāh, the Lord, and Master of all that exists. The One who commands us to follow His straight path. The One who forbad us from following the paths of the people of Hell. I openly testify that none has the right to be worshiped in truth except Allāh alone who has no partners. I also openly testify that Muḥammad is His servant and last messenger. He is the one who conveyed the clear message. He said,

فَعَلَيْكُمْ بِسُنَّتِي وَسُنَّةِ الْخُلَفَاءِ الرَّاشِدِينَ الْمَهْدِيِينَ

"So, you must keep to my Sunnah and to the Sunnah of the Khulafa ar-Rashideen (the rightly guided caliphs), those who guide to the right way."

May Allāh raise his rank, the rank of his family and companions who learned the religion from him and conveyed it to the Muslims; and May Allāh bestow abundant peace upon them all.

To proceed:

O, People! Have Taqwā of Allāh (سُبْحَانَهُۥوَتَعَالَىٰ) and cling to the path in a correct manner which will take you to the abode of peace (Paradise), and be wary of the deviated paths that will lead you to destruction and sin. Understand that the fifteenth night of Shʿabān or its day has any special virtue over any of the days and nights of the year.

So, whoever regularly performs the night prayer throughout the year, then he should do so on this night (the 15th night of Shʿabān) as he would normally do. Likewise, whoever regularly fast the *white days* (i.e., the 13th, 14th, and 15th day of the month) of every month, then he should do so as he normally does. Likewise, whoever regularly fasts on Mondays and Thursdays every week and the 15th day of Shʿabān falls on one of those days, then he should fast as he normally does. Also, whoever regularly fast most of the month of Shʿabān as reported by Muslim on the authority of ʿĀʾishah (رَضِيَٱللَّهُعَنْهَا) who said,

وَلَمْ أَرَهُ صَائِمًا مِنْ شَهْرٍ قَطُّ أَكْثَرَ مِنْ صِيَامِهِ مِنْ شَعْبَانَ كَانَ

يَصُومُ شَعْبَانَ كُلَّهُ كَانَ يَصُومُ شَعْبَانَ إِلاَّ قَلِيلاً

"and I never saw him observing (voluntary fasts) more in any other month than that of Shʿabān. (it appeared as if) he observed fast throughout the whole of Shʿabān except a few (days)."[5]

And in another wording,

كَانَ يَصُومُ شَعْبَانَ إِلاَّ قَلِيلاً

"He used to fast (all) of Shʿabān except a little."[6]

So, whoever emulate the Prophet (ﷺ) in fasting most of Shʿabān and the fifteenth day passes by then there is no problem because in this situation he is acting according to the Sunnah.

What has been prohibited though is specifying this particular day. O servants of Allāh! Understand what has been firmly established by the Prophet

---

[5] Saḥīḥ Muslim No. (1156).
[6] Sunan an-Nasāʾī No. (2179).

(صَلَّالَلَّهُعَلَيْهِوَسَلَّمَ) of supererogatory acts of Ṣalāh and fasting is a treasure for the Muslim and abundant good. So, it is impermissible for the Muslim even to consider other than that of strange matters, acts of innovation, and reports which haven't been firmly established. Indeed, this way is that of the people deviation who follow unclear matters over clear ones; those who revive acts of innovation and do not revive acts of Sunnah.

So, have Taqwā of Allāh and understand that the finest speech is the Book of Allāh so cling to it; and the best guidance is the guidance of Muḥammad (صَلَّالَلَّهُعَلَيْهِوَسَلَّمَ) then emulate him. The evilest of affairs are the newly invented ones so avoid them. Indeed, every newly invented matter is an innovation, and every innovation is a misguidance, and every misguidance is in the Hellfire.

Printed in Great Britain
by Amazon

20114369R00058